T0272955

# California Fruits, Flakes & Nuts

## True Tales of California Crazies, Crackpots and Creeps

David Kulczyk

CRAVEN STREET BOOKS

Fresno, California

*California Fruits, Flakes & Nuts*


Published by Craven Street Books
An imprint of Linden Publishing
2006 South Mary Street, Fresno, California 93721
(559) 233-6633 / (800) 345-4447
CravenStreetBooks.com



ISBN 978-1-61035-194-2

135798642

Printed in the United States of America
on acid-free paper.

Library of Congress Cataloging-in-Publication Data

Kulczyk, David.
California fruits, flakes, and nuts : true tales of California crazies, crack-pots and creeps / David Kulczyk.
pages cm

ISBN 978-1-61035-194-2 (paperback : acid-free paper)
1. Eccentrics and eccentricities--California--Biography. 2. Dissenters--California--Biography. 3. Artists--California--Biography. 4. Criminals--California--Biography. 5. Inventors--California--Biography. 6. California--Biography. I. Title.

CT9990.K85 2013
920.0794--dc23

2013028344

*This book is dedicated to*
*Alison Milne Shurtleff*
*(1958–2012)*
*crime aficionado, editor, friend*

# Contents

## Only in California

# Acknowledgments

Alison Milne Shurtleff edited my earliest drafts of this book. Sadly, she died of cancer on February 22, 2012. Her knowledge, humor, and enthusiasm for the macabre, the criminal, and the odd were unsurpassed. I miss her every single day. I would like to thank Eric Schumacher-Rasmussen, who picked up the ball after Alison died and edited this book. I would also like to thank Lorraine Clarke, James Kulczyk, Luke Suminski, John Massoni, Susan Kendzulak, Richard Sinn, James Van Ochten, Nick Miller, John Russell, Mark Staniszewski, Jaguar Bennett, Kent Sorsky, Tobi Shields, Brett "Sadam" Lempke, and professors Joseph Palermo and Joseph Pitti of California State University, Sacramento. And, as always, I thank my wife Donna for giving me the time, space, and patience to do this project.

# Introduction

*Why are Californians like a bowl of granola?*
*Because what isn't a fruit or a flake is a nut.*
*—Anonymous*

That little chestnut about the citizens of California has been around since James Caleb Jackson invented the tasty whole grain cereal back in 1863. You always had to be a little crazy to move to the Golden State. Mountains, deserts, and the Pacific Ocean render it geographically distant from the rest of the world. It borders the large and empty states of Oregon, Arizona, and Nevada, where even a gas station can be more than a tank of gas away. California attracts those who dare and those who are willing to take a risk.

If we were to accept some historians' sugarcoated version of the nonnative founders of the Golden State, you would think that the pioneers were all Bible-reading Caucasians of good personal hygiene who brought civilization to the wilderness. That scenario could not be further from the truth. The majority of people who swarmed to California during the Gold Rush of 1849 were single men, under thirty-years old, came from all over the world, and represented virtually every race, creed, and color. They arrived exhausted from the long journey to California and had little opportunity for personal hygiene. Most found themselves working in unsanitary conditions, and the only safe liquid to drink was alcohol. Combine drunkenness with youthful exuberance, a lack of responsibilities as a result of being thousands of miles away from home, and freedom from social stigma, and you have a recipe for zaniness. Paupers became millionaires and millionaires became paupers, but, in the long run, most forty-niners were just lucky to break even.

Many of the migrants noticed that there were countless opportunities to make money in California. If you had some sort of education, or pretended you knew what you were doing, the sky was the limit in the Golden State. It is still that way.

There have been multiple gold, land, job, and health rushes throughout the Golden State's history. Today, lenient marijuana laws are starting a "Green Rush" to California, as Americans swarm to the state to cultivate California's number one cash crop. California is the place where the bubble is first filled, and if something is going to be discovered, it usually happens here.

There is no shortage of fruits, flakes, and nuts in California. The Mediterranean climate encourages immigration, the cities welcome it, and, for the most part, the people overlook it. The immense geographical size of the state is sufficient to house every brightly burning bulb in the world. The brightest bulbs sometimes burn out the fastest, but there is always another ember waiting to be reignited.

In this book, I chose not to write about the well-known California nutjobs like Emperor Norton, Sarah Winchester, and Charlie Manson, as their stories have been widely told. I wanted to write about the obscure, the scandalous, and the infamous: the Bohemians and inventors who were laughed at during their era; the beloved actors, musicians, and artists who are admired despite their questionable personal flaws; the criminals whose horrifying deeds have become forgotten as their victims' loved ones pass away.

Despite all the hoopla, there is not a place on Earth where you will find so many people of different cultures living side by side, in relative harmony, than in the great state of California.

*"In Los Angeles, all the loose objects in the country were collected as if America had been tilted and everything that wasn't tightly screwed down had slid into Southern California."* —*Saul Bellow*

# Pioneer Crazies

*Before anyone knew there was gold in the hills of California, you could count the nonnative, non-Californio population on your fingers and toes. Then, within two years, thousands of people from all over the world came to the Golden State to try their luck in the search for gold. Most came up empty, but stayed anyway, doing whatever they could to make their way. Thousands of miles away from home and family, some achieved success, while others fell into a dark abyss of insanity, violence, and crime.*

# Chapter 1

## Grizzly Adams

### John Adams—Arnold, Calaveras County

When people think of John "Grizzly" Adams, they usually think of the television program, *The Life and Times of Grizzly Adams*, which aired on NBC from 1977 to 1978. Adams, who was portrayed by stuntman, animal trainer, and actor Dan Haggerty, goes about his mountain man business, accompanied by his tame grizzly bear, like a Gold Rush version of Saint Francis of Assisi. The handsome Haggerty depicted Grizzly as having a psychic connection with all of the animals in the forest. The reality was much different.

Born, raised, and buried in his home state of Massachusetts, Adams was a middle-aged cobbler who worked for his father. In 1849, knowing there was a demand for leather boots in the Wild West, Adams, with help from the family business, crated up a load of shoes and boots to ship to St. Louis, the last vestige of civilization before the wilderness. Unfortunately for the Adams family, the entire shipment was destroyed by fire while being warehoused in St. Louis.

Adams used the fire as an excuse to travel to Missouri to inspect his damaged commodities. He continued traveling west, abandoning his wife, children, and his father's shoe company. Adams took the torturous southern route to California, through Mexico and the Sonora Desert, arriving in Stockton in 1849.

A poor businessman, Adams tried his hand at various enterprises, becoming a cattle rancher, tavern owner, and gold miner, and failed at all of them. He was taken to court numerous times, always coming out on the short end of the decision. At a time when land squatting was the

## The Last California Grizzly

The last known wild California grizzly bear was killed on October 15, 1926, in Tulare County by J.W.C. Rice. The bear rendered seventeen gallons of lard.

norm, Adams got kicked off of the property on which he was squatting. One of his problems was that he would start a business and then leave it to a hired man to manage while he went on to a new enterprise.

Adams found success live-trapping the grizzly bears that freely roamed the state. The grizzly bear is a fearsome creature that can weigh over a thousand pounds and stand seven feet tall on its hind legs. A grizzly's claws are as long as human fingers and they can easily rip a man's head off with one swipe of the beast's massive paws. Even the California aboriginals stayed clear of the grizzly.

There was an incredible lack of entertainment during the early years of California, and bearbaiting was one of the biggest events available. Weary miners would come down to town to drink and watch the horrific spectacle of a captured grizzly being forced to fight a bull within an enclosed area. The result was an orgy of blood and gore.

To capture grizzlies, Adams would build a thick log trap and bait it with a calf. A bear would walk into the trap and a heavy gate would slam shut behind it. The beast would stew in the trap while Adams arranged for a buyer. When the sale was made, the trap would be loaded onto a cart and driven to town, where the bear would face its violent demise.

Adams could not win for losing in California, suffering defeat in court cases and losing property to slickers and bribed judges. Yet instead of returning home to his family like thousands of forty-niners ultimately did, he kept going farther into the Sierra Nevada Mountains, until he found himself so far away from people that his only neighbors were a tribe of natives. Adams got along with and respected the natives, and they liked him.

Adams trapped all kinds of wild animals for the live animal trade that boomed back on the eastern coast of America. People back East were thrilled to see the exotic sea lions, grizzly bears, and mountain lions of the West. He also sold pelts and meat. Soon, Adams had a menagerie of animals that he took into various mining towns and charged people to view.

In 1853, Adams' brother, William, rode into Grizzly's camp. William, a successful miner, was heading home to Massachusetts when he finally found his brother. He financed an expedition in which Grizzly would collect various live animals, and he arranged for the animals' shipment back to the East Coast.

Grizzly Adams traveled as far as Montana to trap animals. With a couple of helpers, two of them native boys, he shot or captured any animal that interested him.

Adams developed a new and simpler method of capturing grizzlies. He would find a den in the springtime, cause a disturbance, and when the sow came out to see what the noise was, he would shoot her multiple times until she was dead. He would then capture the cubs and take them back to his camp, where he would tie them to a tree and beat them into submission.

Adams was always getting injured by sows that weren't quite dead, and he would often have to finish them off with his Bowie knife. His method of cleaning his wounds was to pour ice-cold stream water on the injury. He claimed it was the best cure.

## Pre-Grizzly

Before he portrayed Grizzly Adams in the popular 1970s television program, Dan Haggerty worked as a stuntman on the television show *Tarzan* and built the legendary American flag chopper for the 1960s counterculture film, *Easy Rider*.

On his Montana excursion, Adams captured two grizzly cubs that he kept as pets. Ben Franklin and his favorite, Lady Washington, eventually became tame enough to run alongside Adams' wagon, carrying their own packs—but they were still wild enough to attack their owner. Adams was attacked by his bears so many times that his skull was cracked and his brain exposed.

In 1857, Adams brought his menagerie to San Francisco for an exhibition. It was very popular for a time, but by May 1859, Adams was sued for back rent. In January 1860, Adams secured space on

## Thick Skin

By the turn of the twentieth century, grizzly bears were rare in California; nevertheless they were still hunted. The bodies of these old bears often had generations of weaponry—arrowheads, spear points, musket balls, and rifled bullets—stuck in their hides and tough muscles.

the clipper ship *Golden Fleece* and sailed his zoo to New York City to meet with P. T. Barnum, the great showman.

Barnum saw a man who looked much older than his forty-seven years. Grizzly's beard and hair were pure white, and his skin was that of a man who had lived outside for twelve years. Then there was the hole in his skull. Barnum offered him a deal for his animals and let him stay on for a short tour through the Eastern Seaboard.

Adams later went home to Massachusetts to his wife, whom he had not seen since 1848, and he died there a few months later.

# Chapter 2

## Psycho Hooker

### Ida Brewer—Sacramento

Ida Brewer was a young woman who, in 1853, plied her trade as a prostitute at a bordello run by Annie Woods on Sacramento's Second Street, in what is now part of Old Sacramento State Historic Park. At the time, "Old Sac," as it is known locally, was where all of the action in the city occurred. In addition to being the hub of transportation for the Central Valley, it also served as its center for vice.

On October 20, 1853, Ida learned that a fellow prostitute, Mary Lee, was seeing her favorite client, whom she considered to be her man. Along with her friend, Augusta Dennison, she went to the Second Street house of ill-repute where Mary Lee worked.

Brewer cursed out the timid Lee and demanded that she step outside to settle the dispute. Lee told Brewer that she would never see her man again, but that wasn't good enough for Brewer. She slapped Lee across the face and a full-blown fight ensued. Brewer, not wanting to be beaten by Lee, pulled out a brand-new, eighteen-inch Bowie knife and stabbed Lee in the thigh and abdomen. Lee died twenty minutes later in a pool of blood.

Brewer's two-day trial started the day after Christmas. The jury must have been in a holiday mood because they acquitted her of any wrongdoing. Maybe Brewer's being one of a handful of Caucasian females in California had something to do with it.

If there were such a thing as anger management classes back in the 1850s, Brewer would have been a perfect candidate for the training. On December 12, 1855, Ida flew off the handle again, slashing a customer's throat with the same Bowie knife she had used to kill Lee two years earlier. Picking up a nearby pistol, she shot another man in the chest. The men staggered out into the street, one of them screaming "I'm dead!" before falling, mortally wounded, onto the muddy, manure-covered ground.

Ida Brewer was tried by the court and found guilty. She was fined and told to leave Sacramento. She moved to the gold camp of Dutch Flats and continued to ply her trade.

# Chapter 3

# The Geek

## Tom McAlear—San Francisco

San Francisco in 1849 was a rough-and-tumble town, carved out of the sand dunes that once surrounded it. The rapid growth and rising real estate demand of the city created some decrepit and dangerous neighborhoods, but no place in San Francisco, and maybe the United States, was more demented than the Sydney-Town/Barbary Coast area on the southeast side of Telegraph Hill.

British convicts who had escaped from Australia—then a penal colony for Great Britain—took the neighborhood by force from Chileans, who had set up a tent city on the southeast slope of Telegraph Hill. Soon, every possible vice could be found there: opium, booze, and prostitution. Some taverns had nude waitresses, live sex shows, and wild animals, which were tied up in front of the establishments. People literally took their lives into their own hands just by walking into one of these businesses. It was common to have one's drink laced with a knockout drug, only to wake up far out to sea on a sailing ship. Once at sea, it was either work or be thrown overboard. The phrase "shanghaied" comes from this practice, because Shanghai, China, was the first place in which a sailor could catch a ship back to San Francisco.

The Barbary Coast had its share of revolting drunks, pimps, and whores; however, the most repulsive of the repulsive was Dirty Tom McAlear. Dirty Tom hung out at one of the lowest dives in Sydney-Town, the Goat and Compass, where he displayed his truly revolting personality. For a nickel, he would eat or drink anything handed to him: dirt, feces,

## The Barbary Coast

San Francisco's Barbary Coast existed as a neighborhood of debauchery for sixty-four years. From 1849 to 1913, the district was in essence a lawless area where bars, brothels and dope dens stayed open twenty-four hours a day. Many prostitutes were essentially slaves and never left the area once they entered. When the soiled doves were too sick to attract Johns, they were dosed with opium or alcohol and sent to the cribs in the basements of the bar. There, in dark four-by-six foot makeshift rooms, a customer could spend a quarter to have sex with an unconscious dying woman.

body fluids, bugs, rodents, animal waste—nothing was too appalling or off-limits to the drunken British subject.

In 1852, after he was arrested for "making a beast of himself," Dirty Tom told a court of law that he had taken his last bath when he lived in England, fifteen years before. He also testified that he had not been sober for at least seven years. Not much is known about what became of Tom McAlear after 1852, but it is fairly easy to guess that he did not live a long life.

# Chapter 4

# Psycho Politician

## David Terry—Stockton/San Francisco/Lathrop

California has always been known for its wacky politicians. From captains of industry, with their hands in the treasury, to washed-up actors, the Golden State never fails to amaze the rest of the world with its choices in government. Perhaps the greatest crank who ever held public office in California was the psychotic southerner David S. Terry.

Terry was born in Kentucky in 1823, and his family moved to Texas when he was ten years old. Texas at the time was the northernmost state of Mexico. Terry claimed to have played a man's part in the Texas War of Independence, but he would only have been an adolescent at the time, and it is very unlikely that he saw any action, although he was no doubt affected by the conflict.

Terry did see action in the Mexican-American War, first as a Texas Ranger and later as a private in the First Regiment of Texas Mounted Volunteers. He was involved in the Battle of Monterrey, and later he enjoyed reminiscing about shooting Mexicans from rooftops.

After the war, Terry went back to Texas, studied law, and passed the bar exam. With the news of the discovery of gold in California, he packed up and moved to the Golden State, knowing that where there is money, there is a need for attorneys. Terry hung his shingle in the growing city of Stockton, the distribution center for the southern mines.

Courtroom proceedings in Gold Rush–era California were as wild as the drunken miners who came to the makeshift taverns in the hastily built towns in the canyons. It was not unusual for attorneys to pull guns and knives on opposing council in the middle of a hearing. Fistfights would break out among the spectators, who often placed bets on who would win the grievance. Terry, who was known for his fiery temper, often pulled his huge Bowie knife out of its sheath in the courtroom.

Along with his law degree and his belligerent personality, Terry also brought his pro-slavery beliefs to California. Terry had political ambitions, and California was on the fast track to statehood. The big debate was whether the new state of California would allow slavery.

Terry got himself elected to the California Supreme Court in 1855 and became the chief justice in 1857. Repulsive as he was, Terry was known to be a fair judge, more likely to side with the common man than with a huge corporation. Yet he was almost hanged by the San Francisco Committee of Vigilance during its takeover of San Francisco in 1856. Terry had been sent to San Francisco by Governor J. Neely Johnson to help settle the dispute between the law-abiding citizens of San Francisco and the thoroughly corrupt city officials and police force. While involved in a running street fight with members of the Committee of Vigilance, Terry pulled out his Bowie knife and stabbed a vigilante. The man did not die; however, Terry was arrested by the vigilantes and held prisoner at Fort Gunnybags for several days. He was lucky to leave San Francisco with his life.

Terry was defeated in his reelection bid in 1859, and he blamed his friend, Senator David Broderick, for his failure. Broderick was in the anti-slavery Free Soil Party and lobbied hard to keep California from becoming a slave state.

A Southern racist hothead like Terry

## Another Dueling Politician

Attorney and Mexican War officer James W. Denver was insulted by an editorial that he read in the Alta California newspaper. He challenged the editor, Edward Gilbert, to a duel. On August 2, 1852, they met three miles northwest of Sacramento, and Denver shot Gilbert dead. Politics being what they are, Denver went on to enjoy an incredibly successful career. Between November 1852 and November 1858, Denver served California as a congressman, senator, and secretary of state and then went on to be the governor of Kansas Territory. The city of Denver is named after him. The duel site is now part of Hagan Oaks Golf Course.

could not let anyone dishonor his good name, so he challenged Broderick to a duel, and Broderick reluctantly agreed. They met just outside the city limits of San Francisco on September 13, 1859. Broderick won the coin toss and had first choice of the dueling pistols. The one that he chose had a hair trigger. Broderick wasn't in the best of health. He was a poor shot and had no hunger to be in a duel. Terry, on the other hand, had a bloodlust and had practiced with a brace of pistols for a week before the duel.

Broderick's weapon went off prematurely, the bullet hitting the dirt not far from Broderick's feet. Terry took careful aim and fired a bullet into the senator's chest. Broderick died a few days later.

Terry had to leave San Francisco in a hurry, and he ran off to his San Joaquin County ranch until cooler heads prevailed. He was eventually acquitted of Senator Broderick's murder, but his political career was ruined.

Being a diehard Southerner, Terry went back to Texas at the start of the Civil War to join the Confederate army. Terry's Civil War experiences are impossible to verify, but it is known that Terry carried with him thousands of dollars for the Southern cause, given to him by Californians with Southern sympathies.

After the war, Terry came back to California, but his murderous reputation and his backing of the Confederacy during the Civil War made him a pariah in Sacramento. He lived in Stockton and continued his law career. He represented anyone, as long as the money was there. His children grew up and his wife died. As he got older, he mellowed out. Gone were the days of shooting off pistols in courtrooms and fistfights in foyers with opposing attorneys. Yet, Terry remained a man of fiery intensity.

In 1884, Terry signed onto one of the most scandalous trials in California up to that time. Sarah Althea Hill claimed that she was legally married to millionaire Senator William Sharon of Nevada. She wanted a divorce and half of his fortune. Hill was probably only interested in getting a quick payoff from the senator, but he called her bluff and let her take him to court.

The trial became all the more scandalous when it was announced that Terry had married Sarah Althea Hill. The trial went on for years and was filled not only with both legal and illegal maneuvering of court procedure, but with knife fights, assaults, contempt of court charges, jail stays, and plenty of media coverage. Sarah's sharp tongue got her admonished by the judge almost daily. William Sharon died in 1885, but the trial continued all the way to federal court.

When the case was dismissed, Terry attempted to assault United States Supreme Court Judge Stephen Johnson Field with a Bowie knife. At the same time, a gun was found in Sarah's satchel. Both Sarah and Terry were given jail sentences.

Judge Field, afraid that the psychotic attorney would ambush him, had a federal marshal, David Neagle, assigned to protect him. Field's intuition proved to be correct when, on August 14, 1889, the two judges found themselves in the same railroad restaurant in the small San Joaquin County town of Lathrop.

Terry approached Judge Field from behind and punched him in the head and face before Marshal Neagle shot Terry dead with two quick shots.

Terry's friends raised a ruckus about the legality of the shooting, but Neagle was found to be within his duty in killing Terry, whose history of violence was reason enough to believe that he would have killed the judge. Terry's son, Clinton, challenged Sarah's rights to his father's estate and kept her in court for years. She ended up insane and penniless, dying on February 15, 1937, after spending forty-five years at the State Hospital for the Insane in Stockton.

# Chapter 5

## Shanghai Chicken

### John Devine—San Francisco

People from around the world have made it their goal in life to move to California and enrich their lives from the harvest of the golden land. Before the completion of the transcontinental railroad on May 10, 1869, the easiest way to get to San Francisco was by sea. Historians basically agree that the sheltering waters of the San Francisco Bay were one of the major reasons that American politicians were so eager to make California a state. The discovery of gold in the Sierra Nevada Mountains in 1848 allowed California to skip over territory status and enter the Union as a state in 1850.

The discovery of gold also brought thousands of ships loaded with cargo and passengers to San Francisco, where there was a shortage of just about everything. Outrageous prices could be had for ordinary objects, as California did not have a manufacturing base and had to depend on imports from other parts of the world. The lure of California gold was too strong for most of the arriving sailors, and, by 1851, hundreds of abandoned ships dotted San Francisco Bay, as not enough men were available, or interested, in manning them. San Francisco was turning into a one-way trip for shipmasters, who often could not hire a crew to sail outbound.

The problem was solved by the age-old crime of shanghaiing, the forcible kidnapping of men to work on ships. It was a simple crime, carried out by men who had no qualms about killing a man who resisted. Usually the shanghaied men, preferably experienced sailors, were unconscious, knocked out with drugs slipped into their drinks or cigars at drinking establishments that catered to seamen. Dumped through a trapdoor onto a dirty mattress, the hapless sailors were kept sedated and confined until they were taken at night to a waiting ship. Sometimes, it would take as much as three years before the shanghaied would make it back to San Francisco.

The men who shanghaied for a living were called crimps and their procedure was diabolical. While an inbound ship waited for a berth at the crowded docks of San Francisco, runners in sturdy Whitehall boats would row up to the ship with rotgut whiskey, cigars, and Victorian pornography to offer the entertainment-starved sailors. If the captain was weak, the runner would board the ship and get the men drunk before convincing them to abandon the ship and enjoy the sins of the City of Saint Francis. Once ashore, they would be brought to a seedy waterfront bar, where they would be given knockout drops in their drink. They would awake to find themselves aboard an outbound ship in the Pacific Ocean.

John Devine was one of the worst crimps in San Francisco. Born in Waterford, Ireland, on June 19, 1840, he arrived in San Francisco around 1860 and was almost immediately shanghaied. Arriving back to San Francisco in 1863, Devine had decided during his long, imposed voyage that he would never go out to sea again.

Devine took up professional boxing as a lightweight under the London Prize Rules. The rules were simple: two men fought bare-knuckled in a ring until one of them could not fight anymore. Biting, gouging, or hitting below the belt was not allowed, but these rules were universally ignored.

Devine picked up the name "Shanghai Chicken" because he was brave and foolhardy, like a Shanghai rooster. The slightly built Irishman was quick with his fists and surprised his opponents with swift uppercuts. The Shanghai Chicken's last fight was against Soapy McAlpine in San Bruno in 1866. It went one hundred sixteen rounds before Devine could not continue.

Touting his reputation as a tough-as-nails fighter, Devine started working as a runner for crimp Johnny Walker. It was the perfect job for his degenerative character and gave him plenty of free time to pursue his other criminal activates as a thug-for-hire, burglar, pickpocket, and pimp.

Devine moved on to work for the king of crimps, Shanghai Kelly. One of the most notorious crimps on the Pacific Ocean, Kelly's saloon and boardinghouse was at 33 Pacific Street. The three-story wooden building was built over the tidal flats, perfect for secret boarding of a Whitehall boat.

## Shanghaied to Shanghai

During the Gold Rush, ship's captains could not hold onto their crews once they docked in San Francisco. The sailors would jump ship and run off into the gold fields and as a result the bay was littered with anchored ships. Enterprising criminals saw a great opportunity. Charging a hundred dollars a head, crimpers would work with San Francisco's bars and boarding houses to supply the ships with unwitting crews. Sailors and ordinary people were rendered unconscious with either a club or opium-laced drink, bundled up and rowed out to waiting ships. The shanghaied men would wake up as the ships were out at sea. They had to work as a crewman or starve. To get back to San Francisco, the shanghaied men, who often found themselves on a ship to Shanghai, had to work their way back as sailors, which sometimes took years.

The greatest story about Shanghai Kelly is when he had a huge order of sailors to fill and had trouble crimping enough men. He sent out open invitations to San Francisco's drunks and riff-raff to attend his birthday party. Kelly rented a ship, the *Goliah*, stocked it with cheap whiskey, allowed ninety men onboard and cast off for an around-the-bay leisure excursion. Soon, the partiers got groggy and passed out. The *Goliah* chugged out through the Golden Gate strait and rendezvoused with several crewless ships, where the unconscious men were hauled aboard. Kelly received ninety dollars a head. As luck would have it, a ship had just docked at San Francisco with the survivors of a shipwreck, and nobody noticed the empty *Goliah*, as it docked at the wharfs.

On one occasion, while Devine worked for Kelly, he convinced a minister that sailors anchored in the bay needed some spiritual guidance. Devine rowed the minister up to a ship and crimped him out to the captain for sixty dollars.

Devine quickly rose to become Kelly's second in command. His area of expertise was to attack competing runners and hijack their kidnapped

## Calico Jim

Notorious 1890s crimp Calico Jim is said to have shanghaied six different San Francisco policemen who were sent to arrest him. They were knocked out, one after another and sold to waiting captains. Years later, after they worked their way back to San Francisco, they officers found out that Calico Jim had left town shortly after they were shanghaied. After getting a tip that Calico Jim was somewhere in South America, they pooled their money together, chose one of the members by lot, and sent him searching for the crimp. After a few months of searching, the officer found him in Callao, Chile. He shot Calico Jim six times, one for every shanghaied officer.

sailors for Kelly to crimp out to sea captains. Devine was not beyond shooting the rival crimp for his quarry.

In 1867, Devine and two other men were accused and arrested for the gang rape and attempted murder of Martha McDonald, a young Scottish woman. After the men were through violating her, they threw her off the bridge at Mission and 16th streets into Mission Creek. McDonald told police that Devine had wanted to kill her, but Devine's accomplices disagreed. The case never went to trial because Martha McDonald was never seen or heard from again.

Devine started to fall out of favor with Kelly and was fired. Devine turned the tables on Kelly by shanghaiing him in the spring of 1868. On June 13, 1868, Devine and his new partner in crime, Johnny Nyland, got word that Shanghai Kelly had been killed in Peru, and the two men hit the Barbary Coast to celebrate.

The Shanghai Chicken and Nyland did not celebrate like normal people. Nyland was carrying a huge knife and Devine was packing a pistol. They commemorated the night by shooting and stabbing innocent barhoppers, while they made the rounds of Barbary Coast nightspots. The two laughed as they burst into several sailors' boardinghouses and beat up anyone they met.

This walking cyclone of violence went on uninterrupted until they entered a saloon attached to Billy Maitland's boardinghouse at Front Street near Vallejo Street. Nyland cleared their path inside with his knife and Devine started shooting at bottles of liquor behind the bar. Maitland heard the commotion and immediately disarmed Nyland of his knife and kicked him out onto the street. As Maitland stepped back into his saloon, Devine pointed his pistol at him. Maitland, with Nyland's knife in hand, lunged at Devine, who raised his left arm in front of himself to protect his throat. Maitland sliced Devine's hand clean off at the wrist. While Devine screamed in pain, Maitland picked him up, threw him out onto the street alongside Nyland, and slammed the door.

Devine sat on the sidewalk holding the stump where his hand had been seconds ago and screamed obscenities at Maitland. The door opened, and Maitland tossed Devine's severed hand onto the sidewalk. Nyland helped his friend to his feet and they stumbled into a drugstore at Pacific and Davis, where Devine politely asked the pharmacist to sew his hand back on before he passed out.

At the hospital, doctors gave him painkillers and wrapped up his stump to heal. Devine had a custom-made prosthetic hook with an extremely sharp point on the end to attach to his stump.

Devine was reduced to petty robberies and theft after his amputation. He was still a dangerous man, but his stamina was weakened by his extended recovery. He may also have become addicted to narcotics during his recuperation. Unable to pay off the proper authorities to continue his life of crime relatively free of retribution, Devine increasingly found himself in front of judges who were tired of the murdering cretin. His bail was being set higher and higher, and it became more difficult for him to raise the cash. The Shanghai Chicken found himself frequently caged in the city jail.

The turning point in the life, times, and crimes of John "Shanghai Chicken" Devine was May 15, 1871, the day he shot August Kamp near Devine's mother's ranch in Bay View. Devine had borrowed money from Kamp and did not want to pay him back. Not only did Devine shoot the young German in front of two witnesses, he also left his hat at the scene of the crime.

Devine was arrested the next morning on the steamer *Wilson G. Hunt*, which was docked at Meigg's Wharf and ready to steam out of the bay. In his pocket was the pistol that he used to shoot Kamp, with two spent rounds in the chambers. Kamp lived for ten more days before dying of infections, but at one point Kamp was well enough to pick Devine out of a police lineup.

The trial was quick and Devine was convicted and sentenced to death. He rediscovered his long-lost Catholic faith while waiting his execution and took his last walk at one in the afternoon on May 14, 1873. Four hundred people received invitations to the execution. He was carried to his burial place with the coffin lid open, to satisfy the curious and to the relief of many.

# Chapter 6

# Voodoo Queen

## Mary Ellen Pleasant—San Francisco

Even in death, Mary Ellen Pleasant has been demeaned. She has been accused of being a procurer, blackmailer, baby farmer, voodoo queen, and murderer, and while the charges may or may not be true, one thing is for sure: Mary Ellen was far from the stereotypical meek female of the Victorian Age. A go-between, corporate spy, and power broker for businessmen during the early days of San Francisco, Mary Ellen was business savvy and well paid for her services. As a result of the work she did for civil rights, she came to be known as "the Mother of Human Rights in California." So much of her life is shrouded in mystery and rumors that the real truth will never be known. Even the year of her birth is speculative. Yet, what is most degrading is the racist nickname attributed to her: Mammy.

Born Mary Ellen Williams in either New Orleans or Boston to a freed Louisianan slave mother and a Cherokee father, Mary Ellen worked as a chef for a well-to-do Boston family. She was a beautiful, intelligent, and charming woman, and in all probability moved easily in Boston's upper crust society because she looked more Caucasian than African. Her most startling physical feature was that her eyes were two different colors, one blue, and the other brown. She passed herself off as a Caucasian to whites and as a Negro to blacks.

Mary Ellen married a wealthy Cuban, Alexander Smith, when she was twenty years old. Smith was a passionate abolitionist, and the couple traveled throughout the South, quietly informing slaves about the Underground Railroad and the freedom that awaited them. When Smith died in 1844, he left Mary Ellen forty-five thousand dollars, a fortune in those days, and he encouraged her to do everything she could to help end slavery.

In 1851, Mary Ellen married John Pleasant, an employee of her late husband, and she continued her work of smuggling slaves out of the South into the northern states and Canada. Unable to keep up with his wife's activism, John Pleasant fell by the wayside. Mary Ellen gave abolitionist John Brown thirty thousand dollars toward his effort to lead an armed slave rebellion. When Brown was captured at Harper's Ferry, after he and his sons had taken over the Federal Armory there, a note was found on his body that was signed "M.E.P." Mary Ellen took the remainder of her money and got on a ship to San Francisco, just in time for the Gold Rush.

In California, Mary Ellen Pleasant's reputation as a chef was so strong that she was able to auction her services. The closing bid ended up being five hundred dollars a month, for cooking only. Her contract stipulated that she would not wash dishes.

Pleasant soon tired of being an employee and opened a boardinghouse for single men. Politicians, bankers, and the ne'er-do-well took rooms at the Pleasant House, where they were fed and taken care of like kings. She saw to their every need, including their vices. Soon Pleasant was receiving stock tips and financial advice from the influential men of the booming new city.

Speculation about blackmail spun around the beautiful woman, speculation that was no doubt race-based. Pleasant was a successful female in an extremely male-dominated San Francisco, and she was an exotic one at that. Given the shortage of women in San Francisco, it wasn't unusual for a prostitute to end up marrying a male from elite society, and Pleasant arranged many of these marriages. Racist views that extend to this day have tarnished Pleasant's reputation with allegations that she was a voodoo queen—as if she needed black magic, and not intelligence, to be successful.

Slavery was still legal in the Southern states, and California had its share of Southern prospectors who brought their slaves with them. Pleasant would help any slave or former slave who came to her, whether in finding employment or a place to live. If an African-American got into trouble, Pleasant would show up in court with an attorney to provide representation.

In one instance, Pleasant interrupted court proceedings as a young African-American was being sentenced to San Quentin. She told the judge not to send him to the notorious prison, because if the judge did so, the young man would be ruined. The judge sentenced the man to prison, but he was pardoned by the governor before he reached the prison gate. The judge fell into obscurity.

The escaped slaves she had aided were grateful for Pleasant's help and would do anything for her, including eavesdropping on their employers' dinner guests for stock tips and gossip that Pleasant could use. She may have frightened the more timid blacks by threatening to put a curse on them if they didn't do what she wanted. Many of the former slaves were just a generation or two from Africa and carried their superstitions with them.

In 1866, Pleasant challenged segregation on San Francisco streetcar lines and won. Her case, *Pleasant v. North Beach & Mission Railroad Company*, was used as precedent in California courts and in many civil rights cases.

Pleasant befriended Thomas Bell, a rising executive at the Bank of California who lived at her rooming house at 920 Washington Street. He shared investment tips with her, and the two of them became richer. Bell was eventually worth fifteen to twenty million dollars.

Bell became enamored of one of Pleasant's girls, Teresa Clingan-Harris-Percy. Pleasant arranged the marriage and then moved in with the couple at a stately mansion at 1661 Octavia Street that Pleasant had designed. The marriage turned sour quickly, and Teresa, Pleasant, and Bell ended up living in different wings of the house. The marriage was not legitimate, as the paperwork was never turned in by the priest who performed the ceremony. Teresa tried to sue for divorce, but since there was no legal document, the relationship became fodder for gossip all over San Francisco. Teresa remained in the mansion and Pleasant ran the household.

Bell wanted children to carry on his name and inherit his wealth. Always the wheeler-dealer, Pleasant arranged heirs for him at fifty thousand dollars a child. There was no shortage of abandoned newborns in

San Francisco, and, over time and as legally as possible, Pleasant came up with five heirs for Bell.

Pleasant helped Bell throughout his life and raised his children, making sure that they got the best education possible, as she had with other important men of the era who had illegitimate children with her girls. Pleasant had arranged many marriages in the female-deficient city and knew all of the San Francisco power brokers' secrets. They paid her well for her help and cooperation.

Thomas Bell began having difficulties with William Sharon, a United States Senator from Nevada and the Bank of California's Nevada agent. Sharon was a shady character who was probably responsible for the downfall of Bell's friend, William Ralston, founder of the Bank of California, and he appeared to have the ailing Bell in his sights as his next target. Pleasant got to him first with a beautiful southern belle, Sarah Althea Hill.

Sharon and Hill hit it off and began an intense love affair, leaving Sharon with little time for scheming. Once Sharon had tired of Hill, she produced a marriage certificate and threatened to sue for divorce. Sharon hit the ceiling, and instead of paying off Pleasant and Hill, he took Hill to court to prove that the marriage never happened.

The scandalous trial was covered by all of the San Francisco newspapers, and the courtroom was packed every day it was in session. Hill was represented by the psychotic attorney and former California Supreme Court Justice David S. Terry. The infamous Terry had killed California Senator David Broderick just outside the San Francisco city limits in a duel in 1859, and he was feared and detested in the city. The trial lived up to the newspapers' expectations, as guns and knives were pulled, fisticuffs broke out, and every sordid detail of the romance came out in court.

Pleasant's name was dragged through the mud during the three-month long trial. She was accused of being the instigator of the entire ordeal, using her voodoo skills to create a love potion that was used on Sharon. Pleasant was smeared by the press as being a voodoo queen, baby stealer, cannibal, madam, and murderer. It was whispered that Pleasant paid for the attorney fees. The press bestowed upon her the racist nickname "Mammy."

The trial went through the court system for years, eventually landing in California's Supreme Court, where it was decided in Sharon's favor. By this time, Sharon was dead. Hill ended up in a mental hospital for the rest of her life.

Pleasant continued to care for the ailing Thomas Bell in his mansion until his mysterious death in October 1892. During the night, Bell fell three stories to his death at his home. Pleasant was thought to have murdered him, but charges were never filed. At the age of seventy-eight, it is unlikely that Pleasant had been the one who killed him.

More lawsuits were filed by Bell's children and Teresa Clingan-Harris-Percy over his will. It is assumed that Pleasant died in poverty on January 4, 1904; however, she must have had money stashed away, as she was buried at Tulocay Cemetery in Napa and not in a potter's field.

# Chapter 7

## Elusive as a Will-o'-the-Wisp

### James Dunham—Campbell

In early May 1896, James Dunham was helping out at his father-in-law's orchard in Campbell, California. While picking fruit, Dunham fell off a ladder and hurt his head. He asked his father-in-law, Colonel Richard Parran McGliney, for compensation and was flatly turned down by McGliney, who looked after an East Coast dairy interest.

The twenty-six-year-old law student must have suffered a severe head injury, as he began acting irrational and irritable. His wife Hattie took their infant daughter and moved back to her parent's farm.

Dunham was at the McGliney place on May 26, 1896, while the Colonel, his stepson James Wells, and hired hand Robert Brisco were away in San Jose. Dunham was there trying to patch things up with his wife, when he snapped. Nobody will ever know what was said, but Dunham strangled Hattie by shoving clothing down her throat.

House servant Minnie Shesler walked in on the scene and was strangled in the same as Hattie . For good measure, Dunham took an ax and split the poor girl's head open. He used the same ax on his mother in-law, Ada Wells McGliney. Dunham also shot Ada a few times just to make sure she was dead.

Colonel McGliney and the other men came home a few hours later. Jim Wells was the first to enter the gore-covered dining room and he put up a fierce fight, but Dunham pulled out a revolver and shot Wells several times in the chest.

The Colonel heard the commotion and ran inside the house. He quickly turned heels when he saw his blood-splattered son in-law with a gun in his hand. McGliney ran into the bunkhouse, where Brisco was cleaning up, and slammed and locked the door. Dunham fired a shot right through the door and demanded that the Colonel come out. Knowing that the situation was hopeless, McGliney opened the door and stepped outside. He was met with a blast from Dunham's pistol. Brisco jumped through a window in the rear of the bunkhouse, but he was quickly shot in the back by the mad law student. Dunham then jumped on a horse and rode off.

Unknown to Dunham, another farmhand, George Schaeble, and a neighbor witnessed the entire incident from the barn. The news of the massacre quickly spread, a posse was organized, and roadblocks were set up throughout the South Bay region.

A rancher named Gates reported to the sheriff of Santa Clara County that he had encountered Dunham not long after the murders. He knew Dunham and was taken aback to see him splattered with blood and with a crazed look in his eye. When Gates got too nosy with his questions, Dunham pulled his revolver out and pointed it at the frightened rancher. Luckily for Gates, Dunham fled, and Gates told the sheriff that Dunham was riding toward Mt. Hamilton.

The rugged topography and dense vegetation of the Diablo Range would make tracking the fugitive difficult. Hundreds of canyons and gullies dot the mountains. It was said that a man could hide ten feet away from searchers and not be seen. Santa Clara County sheriff Robert Langford was anxious to catch Dunham before he could reach the San Joaquin Valley, where he could catch a train or a riverboat and be long gone before they knew it.

Soon, the police had too many independent armed possemen combing the countryside for Dunham. Sheriff Langford asked the public to leave the search to the authorities before someone got hurt. Bloodhounds and professional trackers were sent out around Mt. Hamilton to aid in the search.

Dunham's trail disappeared near Gilroy. His horse was found in a canyon near Bell Station on the Pacheco Pass. He was believed to be hiding in Indian Gulch. *The New York Times* reported that he had been captured in Arkansas. James Dunham seemed to be everywhere and nowhere.

The search for Dunham was abandoned on June 9. The authorities figured that he had made a clean escape.

"He is as elusive as a will-o'-the-wisp," Langford told *The Oakland Tribune.*

Nothing was heard about James Dunham until early May 1935, when WPA workers digging a new sewer line came across a skeleton in Capitola in Santa Cruz Country. Identifying the skeleton, as Dunham was easy as Dunham had extensive bridgework done and his dental chart was still on file at the Santa Clara Sheriff's department.

It appears that Dunham went west while the law was looking east. How Dunham died and who buried him will remain a mystery.

# Chapter 8

# First in Flight

## Lyman Wiswell Gilmore—Grass Valley, Nevada County

From the start, Lyman Gilmore's parents knew their young son was different. Born on a farm in Cowlitz County, Washington, Gilmore shunned farm work and stared at eagles and buzzards soaring over the fields for hours at a time. He loved taking things apart and reassembling them, making him an annoyance on the farm. When he was fourteen years old, Gilmore built an operational six-foot-long steamboat from found parts and scrap.

While living with an uncle near Red Bluff, California, Gilmore built a glider with an eighteen-foot wingspan. Constructed around a bicycle, the glider was towed downhill by a friend on a horse and flew five hundred feet. It would have flown farther, but the friend started hooting and yelling at the sight of the glider flying above him, and when the horse looked to see what the yelling was all about, it got spooked by the glider above and lost the towline. The year was 1891, and Gilmore was seventeen years old.

Gilmore was certain that he could build a flying machine. He successfully prospected for gold in the Sierra Foothills to finance his endeavor. On April 27, 1893, nine years before the Wright brothers' first powered airplane flight, Gilmore had the master drawing of his aircraft design signed, witnessed, and dated. The design was forty years ahead of its time. It had an enclosed cabin, metal skin fuselage, one single, low monoplane wing, and retractable landing gear.

Gilmore's mining ventures led him to invent and patent several types of water pumps and steam engines. He also invented the rotary snowplow, but had his patent stolen when he wanted double the money that was offered to him by interested parties. After this experience, his lifelong distrust of his fellow man began in earnest. His behavior became more eccentric, and he said foolish things, making it difficult for him to be taken seriously by people who could have helped him market his inventions.

Knickerbocker Flat in El Dorado County was where Gilmore found himself on May 15, 1902. Launching down a one hundred-foot chute just south of the Middle Fork of the American River, Gilmore's twenty-horsepower, steam-driven airplane took off into the sky, a full seventeen months before the Wright brother's flight in Kitty Hawk, North Carolina. He eventually made more than twenty flights out of Knickerbocker Flat, and his flights covered from one hundred yards to more than a mile. Dozens of people witnessed the flights in the isolated area, and word spread throughout the state, yet few took the events seriously.

Gilmore, being an untrusting semi-hermit, kept his plans secret, and for good reason, as the early twentieth century was a time of backyard inventors and well-funded labs headed by Alexander Graham Bell and Thomas Edison. History is littered with eager inventors who were careless with their ideas. Undercover agents and thugs were sent out to spy on a wide variety of independent inventors all over the world. Acting as fascinated bystanders, the agents would get an inventor talking about his project and hopefully get a tour, or maybe a look at the specs. They were not beyond breaking and entering to get a better look.

Gilmore hunkered down in Grass Valley, and in 1905, he built the first airstrip and airplane hangar in the world, the Gilmore Flying Field. By then, the Wright brothers were recognized as the first to sustain a powered, heavier-than-air, controlled human flight. The brothers were litigious and secretive, and they fought hard for recognition and patent rights to the flying machine. They were privately funded and wanted to reap the rewards of such an earth-shattering invention. Lyman Gilmore wanted to cash in, too, and he believed that the advanced technology of the enclosed cabin, gyroscopic balance, and monoplane wing would put him high above the other inventors.

In his haste to prove that he indeed had an advanced flying machine, Gilmore let his guard down and allowed Jack Northrup and John Montgomery to inspect his aircraft. His plans were stolen, and soon the

Wright brothers, Glen Curtis, Northrup, and Montgomery were using technology that Gilmore had invented.

Gilmore spent years in court trying to get his invention recognized. To pay for attorneys and his aircraft, he prospected for gold in the many claims in which he held interest around Grass Valley.

In 1909, Gilmore brought his airplane to the California State Fair in Sacramento. It was the first year that the fair was held at its new grounds on Stockton Avenue. Gilmore could not get the plane to start, and he told the disappointed crowd that it would be ready the next day. Suspiciously, the plane was stolen that night and was later found completely destroyed.

The next year, in an effort to appease his investors, Gilmore held an exhibition at his field, but the crankshaft broke and the flight was cancelled. Angry investors and spectators stomped off the field. After that, Gilmore divided his time between his mining claims and his airplanes. He started work on a huge monoplane that looked exactly like a modern airplane. It never flew, but Gilmore continued working on it in his hangar. He built a smaller monoplane around 1911, and had some success with it. Many people argued that the plane flew fine; it was Gilmore's insistence on piloting his aircraft that was the problem.

In 1935, a mysterious fire burned down Gilmore's airplane hangar, destroying his planes and tools. At the same time, Gilmore's home was purposely torched, destroying a lifetime of drawings, notes, and records. Gilmore claimed that he knew who the arsonist was, but refused to identify him. Nobody was ever prosecuted for the crime.

Gilmore went back to mining full-time, knowing that he was lucky to have escaped with his life from the powers that ruined him. He vowed that he would take his secret of flight to his grave. He quit shaving, bathing, and cutting his hair. He wore a long, faded frock coat, even in the summer heat. He became the muttering town nut.

In early February 1951, Gilmore suffered a major stroke and was taken to the Nevada County Hospital in Grass Valley. The reeking man was bathed, and his hair and beard were shaved. His dirty frock coat was thrown into the building's furnace. After Gilmore died, on February 18, 1951, that the reason he constantly wore his filthy coat was discovered. He had sewn thousands of dollars into its lining.

# Chapter 9

## Crazy Cowboy

### C.M. Jones—Sacramento

By 1925, forty-year-old ranch hand C. M. Jones had spent too much time working on J. W. Williams' ranch near Zero, in Yolo County. Jones was paranoid, fearing that there was a plot against him that was headquartered at the Crocker Art Museum in Sacramento. Fearing for his life, he always carried an ax handle with him whenever he went to Sacramento. Williams, his African-American employer, solved the problem by finding chores that would keep him safely on the ranch. But Williams was only his employer, not his warden, and he couldn't keep watch over Jones twenty-four hours a day.

On June 4, 1925, Jones stopped by the museum with his ax handle in hand and asked the caretaker, M. C. Powell, "Are there any Germans inside?"

Powell ignored the cowboy.

"If you got them, I want them," Jones said before he left.

The next day was a sunny Friday, and Jones decided to take care of his delusions. He traded a shotgun for an old .38-56 caliber rifle and ammunition at a Sacramento pawn shop. He went to the Crocker Art Museum and confronted Powell again.

"Show me the way through this place," demanded Jones, as he fired the gun wildly, narrowly missing Powell. Powell ran into the building as Jones continued randomly shooting his weapon.

Richard Brunett and Charles Simonson were in Sacramento on business. The two men had met for the first time earlier that day and decided to visit the museum together while they waited for their trains back to their respective homes. They were just leaving the museum when they walked right into the ranch hand. Simonson tried to grab the rifle away from the husky Jones, but the madman was too quick for him. The seventy-year-old Simonson tried to run, but got a bullet in his chest. He died instantly. Jones stepped back into the foyer and started taking pot shots at pedestrians.

A blacksmith, O. L. Brainard, stepped outside of his shop, the Peerless Iron Works, which was across the street from the museum, when he heard the gunfire. Seeing the gunman on the porch of the Crocker, Brainard stepped back inside to retrieve his shotgun. As Brainard peeked around the door, he saw Jones pointing his rifle directly at him. Brainard shot first and hit Jones, who was fifty yards away. The buckshot buried itself deep into Jones' shoulders, chest, and mouth. By chance, one pellet hit Jones directly in his heart, killing him.

At first, nobody knew the gunman's identity, so the *Sacramento Bee* ran a photo of the dead man on the front page of that evening's paper. J. W. Williams saw the photo and identified Jones.

In the old foyer of the Crocker Museum, you can still see a bullet hole in a closet door from that bloody day.

# Chapter 10

## It's a Gas!

### Edna Fuller—San Francisco

The 1920s have been mythologized as the Jazz Age, a time of prosperity and cultural experimentation. If you believe F. Scott Fitzgerald, the cities were full of speakeasies where women in short skirts and men wearing makeup danced to wild jazz music. Everyone drove slick roadsters and had a great time.

Not everyone in the twenties lived the Jazz Age fantasy, of course, and certainly not the Fuller family. Otto Fuller was trying to support his family of seven as a night watchman, earning sixty-five dollars a month. The rent on the Fullers' tiny basement flat at 1376 3rd Avenue in San Francisco was thirty-five dollars a month. Otto and his twenty-nine-year-old wife Edna had moved their brood from Oakland early in 1926, possibly so Otto could be closer to his job.

Five starving children in a basement apartment can make for a very noisy place. Their landlord, who lived above them, regretted renting to the Fullers and called the police on a noise complaint. Otto was arrested because his crying children were disturbing the peace. The couple was ordered to appear in court with their children on August 31, 1926. It was the first step to make the children wards of the state. To make matters worse, the landlord raised the Fuller's rent by fifteen dollars a month.

As Otto left for work on the evening of August 30, 1926, Edna told him, "Don't you worry. Otto. I've found a place for myself and the children."

Otto went to work and did his job just like any other night, and returned home as the rest of San Francisco was just waking up or, in the case of the more freewheeling residents, going to bed. Before Otto even got to his front door, he could smell the strong odor of natural gas. What he found inside made police officers cry. Edna had sealed up the few windows in the three-room apartment after the children were asleep and turned on the gas oven.

The panic-stricken Otto had the mind to telephone the police, and patrolman Fred Krache responded in seconds. The heroic policeman carried all five of the emaciated children down the street to the University of California emergency hospital.

Ten-year-old Georgette, nine-year-old Glenwood, four-year-old Norma, and two-year-old Eniston, along with Edna, were all pronounced dead on arrival. Winfield, Otto's son from a previous marriage, was barely alive. He was put on oxygen and given blood transfusions. Otto himself gave blood for the eleven-year-old, but the boy died the next day.

The entire city of San Francisco was shocked over the tragedy. Police captain John J. O'Meara told the press that he had sought to obtain aid from charity associations for the family two weeks earlier, but the investigator who had visited the home reported that their case did not come within the jurisdiction of his association.

San Francisco morticians donated coffins for the family and one funeral home provided the viewing and services free of charge; thousands of mourners and curiosity seekers went to view the bodies. Otto's family was laid to rest in Cypress Lawn Cemetery in a plot donated by the cemetery.

Otto was too distressed and weak from giving too much blood for transfusions to be able to attend the funeral.

# The Rise of Southern California Nutjobs

*Southern California has always had a grudge against Northern California. For the first seventy-five years of statehood, most of the population, money, and power was based in San Francisco. The primarily Protestant pioneers were a sober and stern group, and they made no bones about their dislike of Catholics and foreigners, who were usually one and the same. To attract more Protestant Anglo settlers, the Southern California bigwigs advertised in Midwest newspapers and magazines to entice older conservative farmers to sell their farms in Indiana and move to warm, beautiful Southern California, where you could pick your own fruit off your own trees. The Midwesterners came by the thousands, bringing along their loose screws and their elevators that didn't go all the way to the top floor.*

# Chapter 11

## Death by Ostrich

### Billy Ritchie—Los Angeles

By 1916, Charlie Chaplin was the most recognizable person in the world. In the age of silent films, subtitles could be easily translated and in most cases, especially with Chaplin's Little Tramp character, body language told the story and delighted audiences from America to Russia. There were all kinds of merchandise, such as dolls and toys, with images of the Little Tramp, and Chaplin look-alike contests were a global phenomenon. There is an old Hollywood yarn that Charlie Chaplin himself entered one of those contests—and did not win.

While look-alikes were happy to receive prizes for winning contests, Chaplin had many imitators in film and stage who wanted to cash in on his style. Billy West, Stan Laurel, and Bert Wheeler all imitated Chaplin when they were trying to make it big any way they could. Chaplin sued one imitator who was bold enough to call himself Charles Aplin. Billy Ritchie was another Chaplin impersonator; however, Ritchie claimed that Chaplin stole the Little Tramp character from him.

Ritchie was born in Glasgow, Scotland, in either 1874 or 1878, and he seemed to have been on stage his entire life. His parents were stage actors who saw to it that Ritchie received formal training at England's oldest theater, the Theatre Royal at Plymouth. He claimed to have originated Chaplin's "slide and wobble" while playing the drunken father in the plays *Ten Nights in a Bar-room* and *Night in an English Music Hall*. Sporting a derby hat, cane, and long-tailed jacket, Ritchie performed his act all over Europe and North America. He even maintained that he originated Chaplin's trademark makeup.

As a member of the popular Karno Fun Factory and Comedy Troupe, Ritchie came to America with Stan Laurel and Charles Chaplin in 1910. Crotchety, arrogant, and fifteen years older than Chaplin, Ritchie could well have originated the Little Tramp character in English beer halls while Chaplin was just a babe in arms, and Ritchie had no problem expressing this to the press.

Ritchie never had much of a chance to challenge his old stage mate. In 1914, he signed a contract with Henry "Suicide" Lehrman's L-Ko Comedy films. Lehrman was notorious as an injury-plagued director and producer who cared little about the physical well-being of his actors and crew.

In the fall of 1919, while acting in a Lehrman production, Ritchie was attacked by a pride of ostriches in a scene gone wrong. He suffered severe internal injuries, as well as broken bones. He never recovered from his injuries and died at his home at 1200 North McCadden Place, Los Angeles, on July 6, 1921. He was either forty-two or forty-seven years old.

It has been said that Charles Chaplin took pity on Billy's widow and set her up with a job in the wardrobe department of an unnamed studio.

# Chapter 12

## Little Miss Bohemian

### Aline Barnsdall—Los Angeles

The daughter of California oil baron Theodore Barnsdall, Aline Barnsdall was born into extreme luxury. Theodore, a lifelong ladies' man, had a stormy relationship with Aline's mother and wanted to divorce her. She refused, so the rich playboy went about his life as if his wife were just another business expense.

When Aline was a teenager, she traveled extensively with her father and saw the great galleries, museums, and landmarks of the world. She traveled in the same social circles as artists, feminists, and freethinkers, instilling in her a lifelong commitment to nonconformity. Even if she didn't personally believe in a particular cause, she respected the participants and contributed her money and support to them. Aline was especially interested in righting social injustices. She gave anarchist activist Emma Goldman, whom the United States government was trying to deport, five thousand dollars toward her legal fund. The government was not pleased with Aline.

By 1917, Barnsdall had inherited half of her father's estate, and with extravagant homes all over the world, she moved first to San Francisco and then settled in Los Angeles. While living in Chicago, she had tried her hand at acting, but, by the time she moved to California, she was more interested in directing and producing. Her plays drew rave reviews and were heavily attended. Aline was most comfortable in the company of bohemians, and she shocked the conservative upper crust of Los Angeles by getting pregnant by her Polish actor boyfriend. She gave birth on August 19, 1917, and decided to raise her child without going through the tedious bourgeois convention of getting married. She named her daughter after herself, but called her Sugartop.

In 1919, Aline bought thirty-six acres of undeveloped property known as Olive Hill in Los Feliz, a district of Los Angeles. Her intention was to build a community theater complex, with living quarters for artists-in-residence, teaching facilities, and lodgings for herself and Sugartop. At the time, the former hillside olive grove was one of the last undeveloped parcels of land in Los Feliz, and the locals were hoping to make that land into a much-needed park. Barnsdall promised the city that its residents would have access to the facilities. The city okayed the project, mindful of Ms. Barnsdall's reputation for generosity.

Barnsdall hired the irascible architect Frank Lloyd Wright to build her arts center. As usual, Wright was his cantankerous self and the two fought over the design and delays. There may have been a little sex thrown into the mix, but eventually, with the help of other architects, including Wright's son, Hollyhock House and other buildings in the compound were finished in 1926.

Barnsdall, with her fortune to back her up, was a force to be reckoned with in Los Angeles' chic artistic circles. She was prominent in financing the Hollywood Bowl as a place for public entertainment of the arts and was a patron to many artists, architects, and writers. At the same time, she supported perennial Socialist Party candidate and Pulitzer Prize–winning author Upton Sinclair in all of his political bids. She was also a rabid supporter of Thomas Mooney, considered by many to have been railroaded into a conviction for his role in the San Francisco Preparedness Day bombing of 1916. Aline had large billboards posted on the Olive Hill estate exclaiming her political views in an effort to educate her fellow citizens, much to the dismay of her neighbors.

By 1923, Aline tired of Hollyhock and its ongoing construction problems. Frank Lloyd Wright's designs were notorious for their leaking roofs and low ceilings, so Aline started negotiations to turn Hollyhock over to the city of Los Angeles for use as a public library and park. The city wasn't too keen on losing Olive Hill's tax base or maintaining the delicate buildings in its compound. To add to the situation, Barnsdall's donation had strings attached: She forbade any war memorials on the property, and inserted a provision that the California Art Club would have a fifteen -year lease on the main building. Aline further specified that she would stay in a secondary structure, Residence B, for as long as she wished. However, the city reneged on the deal, leading to years of lawsuits and more billboards informing the public about the abuses of the city's government. The city eventually concurred with Barnsdall and took Olive Hill into its trust. More lawsuits were filed by Barnsdall, as the city neglected to maintain the property.

Barnsdall spent the rest of her life raising Sugartop, traveling, collecting art, and supporting the arts in Los Angeles. On December 18, 1946, she was found half-naked and dead in Residence B of an apparent heart attack.

Hollyhock House is a National Historic Landmark and remains a valuable asset to the arts in Los Angeles.

# Chapter 13

## Silent Fall

### Larry Semon—Hollywood

The son of magician Zera the Great, Larry Semon was literally born into the entertainment world. Along with his mother and sister, Semon basked in the glow of footlights throughout the United States and Canada as his father's assistant throughout his childhood years. He was schooled backstage and was a seasoned vaudevillian by the age of twelve, adept in pantomime, singing, and acting. On his deathbed, Zera the Great begged his son to get out of showbiz and pursue art. Semon attended high school in Savannah, Georgia, and art school in New York City, eventually becoming a freelance cartoonist for such newspapers as *The New York Telegram*, *The New York Herald*, *The North American*, and *The New York Evening Sun*.

President Taft was so delighted by Semon's popular, clever cutout cartoons that he requested that Semon draw a caricature of him. Semon enraged magicians all over the world by drawing a series called *Mysteries of Magic, Past and Present, Exposed*. Drawn in pen and ink, the illustrations exposed the tricks of their trade.

In 1913, Semon came to the attention of Vitagraph Studios and, after a few lessons in film pantomime, began acting in shorts, or one-reel comedy films. Wearing heavy vaudeville makeup and a derby hat, Semon had a knack for creating chaos in every film, and the Vitagraph shorts became very popular with the public.

With his success, Semon was able to gain artistic control over his films and soon started writing, directing, and acting in them. His films began incorporating bigger and bigger sight gags, realistic sets, and, for the era, cutting-edge special effects. Rather than use movie sets, Semon built functioning water towers, barns, and sawmills that would be destroyed by the end of the motion picture. Vitagraph renegotiated Semon's contract, giving him more than three million dollars to finance and produce his own films.

Semon came close to rivaling Charlie Chaplin in popularity and was in the same league as Buster Keaton and Harold Lloyd. He started a stock company that included Stan Laurel and, later, Oliver Hardy. After dozens of films together, Semon felt that Laurel was getting too many laughs and fired him.

Indulging himself, Semon spared no expense when it came to the production of his films, but now the money was coming out of his own pocket rather than Vitagraph's, and Semon began having money problems. His creativity was also part of his downfall, as Semon never settled on one distinct character, like Chaplin's Little Tramp or Keaton's Sad Sack. Audiences did not have time to relate to his many characters, which were often not all that different from one another.

In 1925, Semon produced a silent version of *The Wizard of Oz*, with himself as the Scarecrow and Oliver Hardy as the Tin Man. The plot had little to do with L. Frank Baum's original book, and the film was a flop at the box office. Newly married and running low on funds, Semon found himself unable to get financing for his projects. He got work producing and directing short films for Educational Pictures and filed for bankruptcy.

Semon went on the vaudeville circuit to earn some needed cash and suffered a nervous breakdown after months of doing one-night stands. He returned to Hollywood and checked himself into a Victorville, California, sanitarium, where he died from tuberculosis and pneumonia on October 8, 1928, at the age of thirty-nine.

The man who made over one hundred and twenty-nine pictures in thirteen years and was at one time one of the world's most popular silent comics was cremated, his memorial service attended only by his family. There were rumors that Semon used his skills as a magician to fake his death; however, his death certificate was eventually found, putting that rumor to rest.

# Chapter 14

## In His Sister's Shadow

### Jack Pickford—Los Angeles

Nepotism in the entertainment business is as natural as a horse swatting flies with its tail. The children of show business people are usually exposed to the limelight at an early age. In many ways, it is the only thing they know. In this regard, Jack Pickford was beyond fortunate: His sister, Mary Pickford, was the biggest star of the silent film era.

Born in Toronto, Canada, on August 18, 1896, Jack, along with his sisters Lottie and Mary, lit up stages all over North America. Yet right from the beginning, Mary was the star of the family. Their business-minded mother, Charlotte, made sure that any theater producer wanting to hire Mary also had to find parts for her and her other two children. Riding on Mary's coattails, the less-talented siblings found themselves living in Beverly Hills, eating in expensive restaurants and traveling first class.

Jack took up flying when airplanes were little more than motor-powered kites. He did some aerial stunts for films, but he mostly flew drunk, buzzing his sister's and friends' homes and shouting obscenities.

When the United States was dragged into World War I, Jack joined the United States Navy. Banking on the Pickford name, he was stationed in New York City, where his duties included securing hotel suites for officers' weekend parties and making sure that his famous movie star friends, various Broadway chorus girls, and specially selected young starlets attended the functions. Pickford's luxurious apartment was a favorite hangout for naval officers, army brass, and visiting dignitaries.

When Jack wasn't procuring prostitutes for officers, he acted as a go-between, arranging payoffs from rich young men wanting to avoid military duty. Jack would get a cut of the bribe after it went to the right officer. He was caught and dishonorably discharged, and, being the weasel that he was, he gave testimony that implicated his superiors. Mary, who raised millions of dollars for the war effort, used her impressive political influence and her equally impressive bank account to keep the Pickford name out of the media and to get Jack out of his predicament. Several years after the war, Mary even got Jack's military record cleared, securing an honorable discharge for him.

Jack Pickford's Hollywood career petered out after the war. Jack was an above-average actor, but he was forever overshadowed by his superstar sister. Once the war ended, Jack made about one picture a year. He was also on the Pickford payroll, making fifty thousand dollars a year for just showing up when Mary asked him to. Jack constantly borrowed money from his sister, who would give him a stern lecture before giving him a kiss.

Jack's interests ranged from snorting cocaine with showgirls to throwing five-day methamphetamine- and alcohol-fueled parties and to smoking opium with his Hollywood pals. Allegedly, Mary spent a small fortune keeping Jack out of jail and the newspapers.

Jack and the beautiful actress Olive Thomas eloped in 1916. Together, they were the wildest couple in filmdom. Perennial night owls, they were constantly seen at nightclubs and exclusive restaurants. They openly drank alcohol, even though Prohibition was in effect. Their outrageous behavior was fodder for the fan magazines, as neither was shy about his or her antics. Every fight, rumor, and affair was duly reported in the tabloids.

In an attempt to patch up their rocky marriage, the couple took a cruise to Europe. During their month in Paris, the pair slummed in the Montparnasse Quarter and were seen patronizing the seedier bistros, where it was easier to obtain heroin and cocaine.

In the early morning hours of September 5, 1920, the couple staggered into their suite at the Hotel Ritz in a drugged-out daze. Jack passed out as soon as he hit the bed. Olive, allegedly stoned out of her mind, accidentally drank Jack's mercury bichloride, which he used to treat his chronic syphilis. Before penicillin was discovered, the poisonous mercury bichloride was thought to cure the symptoms of the dreaded venereal disease. It was directed to be used sparingly, but Olive, thinking it was either water or booze, took a big swig. Screaming loudly enough to wake half of the hotel, she was taken to the American Hospital in the Paris suburb of Neuilly-sur-Seine, where the beautiful woman suffered a slow and painful death. She died on September 10, 1920.

Jack was devastated by Olive's death. Despite their affairs and fights, they were madly in love with each other. The French authorities performed an autopsy and verified that Olive did indeed die of accidental ingestion of mercury bichloride. The Pickford money machine may have had a say in the procedure, as there was no mention of the drugs Olive was known to take. Heartbroken, Jack Pickford flew back to America and into his usual escapades of drinking, doping, and whoring.

Two years later, Jack married Marilyn Miller, the highest paid musical-comedy actress in the country. Miller, a former Ziegfeld Follies dancer, was also a world-class party girl. Pickford's marriage to Miller was violent, and their affairs and public spats continued to keep Jack on the front pages of the tabloids, much to his prim and proper sister's chagrin. Mary Pickford, who was at the height of her career and the biggest movie star in the world, continued paying off cops, judges, and news editors to keep the more incriminating debauchery of her beloved brother out of the courts and newspapers. Miller divorced Pickford in 1927.

Three years later, Jack married another Ziegfeld Follies dancer, Mary Mulhern. Just twenty-two years old at the time, Mulhern could not handle her syphilitic, drug addicted, alcoholic, and increasingly sadistically violent husband. She wisely left him.

Before you can say divorce, Jack's condition took a turn for the worse. Emaciated and wracked with venereal disease, his liver and kidneys destroyed by drugs and rotgut Prohibition booze, Jack Pickford died on January 3, 1933, at the American Hospital in Paris, the same hospital in which Olive Thomas had died

Jack Pickford's final words were, "I have lived more than most men, and I am tired." He was thirty-six years old.

# Chapter 15

## True Square

### Aimee Semple McPherson—Los Angeles

Born in Canada to a family of followers of the Salvation Army, the evangelical Christian church known for its charitable work, Aimee Semple McPherson became upset in high school over the teaching of evolution in the Canadian school system. After marrying Robert James Semple, an Irish Pentecostal minister, when she was seventeen years old, Aimee and her groom took off for an evangelizing tour of the world. While in China, they both contracted malaria. Aimee, who was pregnant with her first child, Roberta Star, survived. Robert did not, and he was buried in Hong Kong Cemetery. Roberta was born a month later, on September 17, 1910.

While recovering from malaria at her parent's home in Canada, Aimee fell in love with accountant Harold Stewart McPherson, and they married on May 5, 1912. The marriage was not a happy one, and Aimee went on an extended tent-revival tour of Canada and the United States. McPherson faded away from Aimee's life and filed for divorce in 1921.

Joined by her mother, Mildred, Aimee took a convertible Packard automobile, decorated it with religious symbols, and stormed the South, stopping in towns and giving her sermons through a megaphone while standing on the backseat of her car. The collection plate was passed around, and mother and daughter went to the next town and the next.

Sister Aimee, as she now called herself, began to be booked into boxing arenas and auditoriums. For publicity, Sister Aimee paraded around the city in which she was performing with a sign reading, "Knock out the Devil." She involved herself with such sham tricks as speaking in tongues and faith healing. The people clamored to her events for guilt-free entertainment and salvation. It was said that up to thirty thousand followers attended one such event, held in a boxing ring in San Diego.

Aimee started a magazine called *Bridal Call*, writing about women's rights and their responsibility to spread the word of God. She formed the International Church of the Foursquare Gospel and based it in her favorite city, Los Angeles. She attracted attendees by creating a spectacular stage show that was more like a Broadway revue than a church service. By combining existing American culture with fundamentalist Christianity, the International Church of the Foursquare Gospel made going to church as much fun as going to a vaudeville show.

On January 1, 1923, Sister Aimee dedicated the fifty-three-hundred-seat Angelus Temple in Echo Park, which would become home to her ministry. A year later, she was granted a broadcasting license for her own radio station, KFSG-AM, with a powerful fifty-thousand watt transmitter. Sister Aimee's charismatic sermons could be heard all over the Southwest, the West Coast, and in parts of Mexico.

Sister Aimee allowed all racial groups to attend her sermons, where she preached against evolution, alcohol consumption, and the loose morals of young people. Her followers responded by opening up their wallets and purses, making Sister Aimee rich.

On May 12, 1926, Sister Aimee went swimming at Ocean Park Beach, north of Venice, California, and vanished. She was presumed drowned. The press went ballistic, with William Randolph Hearst's sensational *Los Angeles Examiner* leading the media circus. All-night services were held at Ocean Park Beach, with thousands attending the vigils. Her followers mourned, and two men died while searching for her body.

On June 23, Aimee appeared in the border town of Agua Prieta, Mexico, claiming that she had been kidnapped, drugged, and held for ransom by two people. She claimed that she finally was able to escape her captors, walking thirteen hours through the desert.

Authorities were wary about her story. Aimee had been found in pretty good shape for someone who had walked through the hot Sonora Desert in the summertime, and her shoes had grass stains on them. More confounding was the fact that she was wearing her own clothing, including a watch that her mother had given her, when she had last been seen wearing only a bathing suit.

This was not the kind of publicity Sister Aimee was used to. Witnesses from Carmel-by-the-Sea, in Monterey County, claimed they had seen her around town during the time of her disappearance. A grand jury convened in Los Angeles, and Aimee and Mildred gave misleading answers and told outright lies. They were both charged with obstruction of justice.

Nobody believed Aimee's story, and rumors and innuendos proliferated as to why such a public figure would fake her own kidnapping and death. Did she go to Mexico to have plastic surgery or an abortion? Did she run off with a secret lover, or was it just another one of her publicity stunts?

The district attorney decided not to press charges against the minister, and Sister Aimee's long, downhill journey began. No longer the darling of the media, she was ousted from the church she founded. In 1930, she suffered a nervous breakdown. The next year, she married singer David Hutton. The conservative Pentecostals got into an uproar over Aimee's choice of a mate and the fact that her second husband was still alive. Aimee and David divorced in 1934.

Sister Aimee continued her salvation road shows for the next decade, until she was found dead in her Oakland hotel room of an overdose of Seconal, for which she did not have a prescription. Largely considered a suicide, her death was listed as "accidental overdose" by the coroner.

The Foursquare Gospel church was taken over by Aimee's son, Rolf, who led the church successfully for forty-four years. The religion that Aimee founded now claims more than eight million members worldwide.

# Chapter 16

# Grumpy Stooge

## Jerome Horwitz—Los Angeles

His family called him Babe, but he was known throughout the world as Curly, the most popular member of the legendary comedy group, The Three Stooges. The riotous man-child sang silly ditties, had arguments with inanimate objects, danced like he was on air, and could get hit in the head with a monkey wrench with no visible injury.

Born on October 22, 1903, in Brooklyn, New York, Jerome was the youngest of the five Horwitz boys. His parents, Solomon and Jenny, were Jewish immigrants from Lithuania, and they doted on all of their sons, hoping that they would achieve the American dream. Jenny was the engine of the family and became a successful real-estate agent, dealing in million- dollar investments in Brooklyn. She became the neighborhood advice-giver and charity worker, while her weak-willed, country bumpkin husband, Sol, was content to collect rent and make bank deposits. Jenny had high hopes for her children, and she put a lot of pressure on her sons to become doctors, lawyers, or bankers. Every one of her children, except Curly, left home as soon as he could. Two of them, Sam and Moses, entered vaudeville and, along with Larry Fine, joined comedian Ted Healy and toured the country under various names, ending up as Ted Healy and His Stooges. Sam changed his name to Shemp, which is how Jenny pronounced Sam, and Moses first went by Harry and then finally became Moe. Both Sam and Moses went by the last name Howard.

The world knew Curly only as the wisecracking inventor of break-dancing, but his real life was that of a sad and friendless loner. Growing up as the youngest member of the Horwitz family, Curly had no positive male role model in his life. His successful, domineering mother and submissive father confused Curly. His brothers were all much older than he was and he only saw them on special occasions. Jenny didn't want Curly out of her sight, so she hired him to chauffeur her and Sol around on their daily errands. Curly learned about life from the guys he hung out with on the street corners of Brooklyn and boardwalks of Coney Island. He also was a regular at the Triangle Ballroom, where he first did his exaggeratedly spastic, yet graceful, dance moves that would be his future trademark—despite being in pain from accidentally shooting himself in the calf when he was an adolescent.

To Curly, females were something to pursue and conquer with a whistle and a hooting "Hi Toots!" He was never without a female dancing partner, yet whenever he started seeing one special female, Jenny would somehow step in and put an end to it. At the age of twenty-six, Curly secretly married a woman, but once Jenny caught wind of it, she had the marriage annulled and, using her political connections, made sure that no record of the marriage or annulment existed. Hoping to cheer up their son, Sol and Jenny took Curly on a trip to Europe, then left to visit family in Lithuania, leaving Curly on his own in Paris. He had the time of his life.

Curly idolized Moe and Shemp and wanted desperately to get into show business. In 1928, he joined Orville Knapp's band as the comic conductor. He wore a breakaway tuxedo that gradually fell apart as he wildly conducted the orchestra until he was left only in his long underwear. He brought down the house every night.

By this time, Moe, Shemp, and Larry were making a name for themselves with and without Ted Healy, who was showing the effects of a lifetime of high-living and Prohibition booze. Shemp, always a cautious man, decided that he didn't want to work with Healy anymore and took a lucrative acting role as Knobby Walsh in the Vitaphone shorts featuring the comic strip boxer Joe Palooka.

Healy exploded with rage when he found out that he had lost a Stooge, but Moe, who was The Three Stooges' manager, saved the act by recommending that his little brother Curly join the group. Healy saw promise in Curly but demanded that he shave off his thick brown hair and waxed mustache to make his appearance more comical. Curly loved his hair and cried when he came back from the barber.

Moving to Hollywood only improved Curly's social life, and he often jumped on stage at clubs to play the spoons, dance, or finger the upright bass with the orchestra. He was never without a young starlet or two on his arm. Big brother Moe would wait up in his hotel room until he could hear his brother loudly announce his presence. Larry Fine and the two Howards stayed with Healy for ten two-reel comedies shot between 1930 and 1933, before they had had enough of Healy's bad behavior.

## The Third Stooge

Larry Fine was the only Stooge who was a musician. A violinist, he was on his way to a European music conservatory, but the outbreak of World War I put an end to his dreams. Despite his prissy ways, Fine was also a boxer when he was a teenager, winning his first and only professional bout. His father threw the towel in on his boxing career. Larry was a gambler who lost money hand over fist, and like Shemp Howard, he was generous with what money he had. He and his wife, Mable, lived in the President Hotel in Atlantic City, New Jersey, and the Knickerbocker Hotel in Los Angeles for most of their lives and did not buy a home until the late 1940s.

Signing with Columbia Pictures, The Three Stooges exploded onto the movie screens all over the world with their clever two-reel film, *Woman Haters*, a musical in which the entire dialog rhymed. The Three Stooges churned out more than one hundred short films with Curly, many of them classics, like *Punch Drunks*, *Three Little Pigskins*, *You Nazty Spy*, *What's the Matador*, *Hoi Polloi*, *Disorder in the Court*, and *Violent is the Word for Curly*. Their short, *Men in Black*, a parody of the 1934 Clark Gable/Myrna Loy social drama *Men in White*, was nominated for the 1935 Academy Award for Best Short Subject, Comedy.

Curly was living the life of a film star. He partied at all of the Hollywood hot spots and recklessly spent money on whatever he fancied at the moment: homes, fast cars, purebred dogs, and his biggest weakness, women. When Curly wasn't intoxicated, he was a sullen, introverted man. He had no close personal friends and his bed was a revolving door of young Hollywood starlets. In 1937, he married Elaine Ackerman, and they had a daughter, Marilyn, but the marriage was loaded with fights and drama, and by 1940 they had divorced. From that point forward, Curly was on the downswing, drinking, carousing, and eating great quantities of restaurant food. He put on a lot of weight and was continuously paying off underage females not to talk to reporters.

Eventually, Curly informed his brother Moe that he was broke. Moe took over Curly's financial affairs and put him on an allowance. Unlike his kid brother, Moe was a family man, with a house in the Toluca Lake district. Bing Crosby lived across the street. With Jenny now deceased, Moe took over her place as the guardian of Curly.

The budget that Moe put Curly on barely slowed him down. Always restless, Curly continued to overeat and party. Moe and Larry, as well as the production team, all noticed that Curly wasn't as on as he usually was. Never one to memorize his lines, Curly always had to concentrate on every scene. His crazy antics, like his famous "n'yuk, n'yuk, n'yuk" and "woo woo woo" were usually ad-libbed when he couldn't remember his lines. Moe persuaded Curly to see a doctor, but it had little effect on his lifestyle.

After a two-week courtship, Curly married wife number three, Marion Buxbaum. The marriage lasted three months before divorce papers were filed. Buxbaum took Curly for everything he had left.

On May 6, 1946, at age forty-two, Curly suffered a stroke on the set of *Half-Wits Holiday*. He was never the same. He married again, and this time he seemed to find his soul mate. His fourth wife, Valerie Newman, gave birth to their daughter, Janie, in 1948, and this time fatherhood latched onto Curly. He became a proud father and loving husband. He lost weight and tried to keep his blood pressure under control. But too much damage had already been done. Curly suffered at least two more strokes and spent his final years in and out of sanitariums and hospitals until he finally died on January 18, 1952, at forty-eight years of age.

# Chapter 17

## Big Bill

### Bill Tilden—Hollywood

He was the world's number one tennis player from 1920 to 1934. He hung out with Hollywood's elite and wrote three best-selling books on tennis. Yet "Big Bill" Tilden, as he was known, has been largely forgotten by the over-hyped modern sports media.

Born to wealthy, upper-crust Philadelphians, Bill was coddled as a youngster by his mother, who home-schooled him and called the family doctor whenever he sneezed. When Bill was in his teens, his mother died, and he was sent to live with his aunt and cousin, who lived a few blocks away from his parents. Tilden kept a room at his aunt's house until he was forty-eight years old. In short order, both Bill's father and his only surviving sibling died. He redirected his grief and immersed himself into the game of tennis, changing the sport from a country club diversion into the athletic and skillful game it is today.

Tilden looked at tennis as both a physical and a mental game. His backhand return baffled spectators and opponents alike. He was quick to figure out his competitors' weaknesses and capitalize on them, tromping them in spectacular plays. A showy but always fair player, Tilden loved playing to the crowd and would sometimes purposely fall behind his adversary in points, only to rally his game and destroy his fellow sportsman.

Tilden won the men's singles title at Wimbledon in 1920 and again in 1921 and 1930, when he was thirty-seven years old. He won seven U.S. National Championships (later to be called the U.S. Open) and seven U.S.

Men's Clay Court championships. Throughout the 1920s, he led the U.S. Davis Cup team, which won seven titles.

As clean and fluid as Tilden was on the court, he was notorious for his poor personal hygiene. He never bathed or showered and had horribly bad breath. His clothes were always filthy. Big Bill was also an effeminate homosexual with a penchant for teenage boys.

Tilden moved to Los Angeles in 1939, where he socialized and played tennis with Spencer Tracy, Errol Flynn, Joseph Cotten, Greta Garbo, Montgomery Clift, Tallulah Bankhead, and Charlie Chaplin. But the conservative Southern California country club set found out about Tilden's fondness for juveniles and he was banned from giving lessons, his main source of income.

On the evening of November 23, 1946, Beverly Hills police pulled over Tilden in his 1942 Packard Clipper for driving erratically. A fourteen-year-old boy was driving and his pants were undone. Tilden admitted to police that he had had sex with the boy.

Tilden was dismissive of the charges, believing that the authorities would quietly drop the case, as they had probably done before. Besides being a sports star, Tilden was politically connected through his family name and believed that his old East Coast connections would take care of things. He was wrong.

Tilden's case was assigned to Judge A. A. Scott, a commie-hating moralist whose son had represented Joan Barry in a paternity suit against Tilden's friend, Charlie Chaplin. The judge had heard an earful of the debauchery that went on at Chaplin's home and wasn't going to go easy on an adult homosexual who liked teenage boys and was best friends with Chaplin.

Arrogantly believing that he was going to be let off with a fine, Tilden pled guilty, against his attorney's wishes. He took the stand and got caught up in his lies. The judge sentenced him to a year in county jail, effective immediately. He was sent to work at the Castaic Honor Farm and was released after seven months.

Tilden's probation forbade him any contact with minors, effectively ending his career as a tennis pro to the young and rich. Chaplin and Joseph Cotten were the only Hollywood types who dared to associate with him. No longer able to afford a luxury Hollywood apartment, Tilden ended up in a series of seedy rentals, each one worse than the last.

On January 28, 1949, the police showed up at Tilden's apartment to arrest him for making improper sexual advances toward a minor earlier in the day, a violation of his parole. It didn't help Tilden that a family friend, Art Anderson, a teenage male, was visiting when the police arrived. On Tilden's fifty-sixth birthday, he was sentenced to another year at Castaic Honor Farm.

Released on December 18, 1949, just in time for the Christmas holiday, Tilden found himself completely friendless. A few days before his release, the Associated Press voted him the greatest tennis player of the first half of the twentieth century. At about the same time, he was purged from the histories of both his alma mater, Penn State, and the Germantown Cricket Club, where he first learned the sport.

Tilden's friend, Gloria Butler, searched all over Los Angeles for him, finally finding him on a public court, giving a lesson. She rented a duplex for them both, with Tilden living in the upper unit. She fed him and kept him company. During the daytime, Big Bill still played tennis, picking up games wherever he could, just for the fun of playing. He would sometimes drop in on pros, who worked at upscale courts, to play a set or two, but his clothes were always filthy and he would often have to be lent the proper attire. Eventually, his reputation, as well as his body odor, got banned from all of the private courts.

For the fun of the game, Big Bill, along with a couple of former pro tennis players, would sneak into Charlie Chaplin's estate to use his court. Chaplin was in exile in Europe after having been accused of being a communist.

On the eve of what was to be an exhibition tour of Texas, a lead-up to the U.S. Professional Championship in Cleveland, Big Bill Tilden was found dead by his friend, Art Anderson. He was lying on his bed, all dressed to go, his bags packed. The world's greatest tennis player left an estate worth eighty-eight dollars.

# Chapter 18
## The Brat Wagon
### Margaret Rowney—Van Nuys

Like millions before and since, Margaret Rowney moved to California to start a new life. The twenty-seven-year-old widow brought her four children to Encino in 1948 after her railroad worker husband was killed on the job. The Pennsylvania Railroad supplied her with a generous pension. The Baltimore native probably thought that the sunlight of Southern California would wash away the grit that stained her heart.

She developed a stable relationship with Raymond Bennett, a thirty-six-year-old foundry worker who cherished his instant family. Margaret called their wood-paneled station wagon "The Brat Wagon," and she had the children's names painted on both sides of the car. Painted on the driver's side door was "Ray" and "Margie" was written on the passenger side.

In the early morning hours of December 14, 1950, while Ray was working the graveyard shift, Margie braided her long hair around her head and put on her blue jeans and a leather jacket. She roused her children—seven-year-old Peggy, five-year-old George, four-year-old Guy, and three-year-old Thomas—from their beds and got the pajama-clad kids into the backseat of the Brat Wagon. She drove up Mulholland Drive into the Santa Monica Mountains and found a secluded spot under a giant oak tree in Topanga Canyon. Carefully, so as not to wake her sleeping children, Margie took a vacuum cleaner hose and attached it to the exhaust pipe of the Brat Wagon, putting the other end into the passenger compartment.

Police on routine patrol found the car. The engine was out of gas, but still warm. The children in the backseat were tumbled across each other just like sleeping children do. Margie was sprawled on the front seat. There was no note.

The murder-suicide perplexed everyone who knew Margie. Her sister, friends, neighbors, and boyfriend Ray had no idea why Margie would do such a thing. On December 19, 1950, Margie's sister Violet flew to Baltimore with five coffins to be interred in her hometown.

Later that day, the heartbroken Bennett took the family dog Inky with him into the garage at the home that was once filled with joyful noise. He ended his life in the Brat Wagon, exactly like Margie had. An empty bottle of whiskey and a note was found inside the home at 4973 Noeline Avenue. The note made no more sense than Margie's actions: "We would have started where we lost them, but we didn't want to be stopped. We will find the reason."

# Chapter 19

## Fraidy Cat

### Samuel Horwitz—Los Angeles

Better known as Moe Howard's older brother Shemp, Sam was born the third son to Lithuanian Jewish immigrants Jennie and Solomon Horwitz in Brooklyn's Bensonhurst neighborhood. With her thick Latvian/Yiddish accent, Jennie pronounced Sam as Shemp, a name that stuck for his entire life. An attention-seeking prankster from birth, Shemp faked illnesses to get out of chores, cried at the drop of a hat, and was, as brother Moe wrote, "a general creator of disturbances."

As he reached his teenage years, Shemp's easygoing nature and quick humor made him quite popular with the females of Bensonhurst. Like his little brother, Shemp spent more time at the movies or vaudeville houses than in school. He and Moe picked up parts as extras in several one-reel films at Vitagraph Studio. He evolved into a natural comedic entertainer and could sing and play the ukulele like a pro.

When he was eighteen, he and Moe bought an old Pope-Harford automobile for ninety dollars. The car's brakes were questionable, but that didn't stop Moe from giving Shemp his first driving lesson. After driving a few blocks, the brakes gave out and the car crashed into a barbershop, which was thankfully closed that Sunday morning. Shemp never drove again and hated to ride in cars for the rest of his life.

Moe and Shemp put together an act for amateur nights and were soon performing at neighborhood dance halls. The brothers started their careers in earnest with a blackface act at the Mystic Theater for five dollars a day. They soon realized that they were the cleanup act, an act so bad that they are intentionally slotted to clear out the theater. Moe and Shemp didn't care, because they were able to hone their timing and ad-libs to an audience that wasn't paying close attention, building valuable stage skills while getting paid.

By 1917, Shemp and Moe managed to get contracted for both the Loew's and the RKO theater circuits simultaneously. They maneuvered around the unwritten rule that you could only work for one or the other theaters by being in whiteface for Loew's and in blackface for RKO. Their act was interrupted when Shemp got drafted into the army during World War I; a chronic bed wetter, he was discharged after a few months. Back with Moe, the two continued their slapstick, ad-lib filled act as well as working with other actors on the vaudeville stage and for Vitagraph Studio.

In 1922, Shemp and Moe joined up with former Brooklyn buddy Ted Healy for a new vaudeville comedy act that immediately went on tour. They often did their act with Shemp in the audience as a heckler who was funnier than the stage act. Healy would finally call out Shemp, who would stumble on stage to cheers and hoots. Shemp and Moe would then engage in a series of wisecracks and slapstick. Their pure clowning brought the house down every night, and, before long, Healy was earning $3,500 a week. Out of the $3,500, Healy paid Moe and Shemp a miserly $100 each. A short time after the troupe started, Larry Fine was brought into the act and they became Ted Healy and His Three Southern Gentlemen.

In September 1925, Shemp married fellow vaudevillian Gertrude "Babe" Frank. In 1927, their son Morton was born. Shemp and Babe loved to entertain fellow entertainers, and their door was always open to everyone, both struggling performers and successful ones.

Ted Healy and His Three Southern Gentlemen toured the United States extensively until 1927, when Shemp and Ted left to perform in the Broadway revue *A Night in Spain*. The show ran for six months, thanks to Shemp's crazy facial contortions and laid-back style. After the show ran its course, the four teamed up again under the name Ted Healy and the Racketeers. They hit the road with a shtick that this time involved props like ladders, falling curtains, and buckets. Of course, the usual slaps, punches, and pratfalls stayed in the show.

Ted Healy and His Three Southern Gentlemen left the drudgery of the road in 1929 to perform in another Broadway revue called *A Night in Venice*. Directed by Busby Berkeley, the show was a modest hit and ran for seventeen weeks before it joined the Loew's circuit tour. When the show ended, the troupe went west to Hollywood. As a group, they filmed the short *Soup to Nuts*, and then prepared for another Broadway show, *The Passing Show*.

Larry, Moe, and Shemp had grown tired of the alcoholic con man Healy. Healy was still keeping most of the money that the act earned and living the high life in a Connecticut mansion, while Larry, Moe, and Shemp still lived modestly in hotels and apartments when they weren't on the road. The brothers had left the company several times before over money, but had always come back to Healy, who would promise the moon if they rejoined.

During the rehearsals for *The Passing Show*, Healy got into a huge argument over money with the producer and quit, taking his Stooges with him. Shemp, though, was sick and tired of Healy's drinking and bullying, and decided to stay with the show.

Shemp was more ambitious than Moe and wanted to exercise his comedic acting chops. He teamed up with Lionel Standard in a series of popular short films directed by Roscoe "Fatty" Arbuckle for Warner Brothers, but filmed at Vitaphone.

Arbuckle had just been acquitted of murder, but the publicity ruined his reputation. He left the West Coast for New York City, where he directed and wrote films under the pseudonym William Goodrich. Shemp, Lionel, and Fatty/William filmed six successful shorts together.

Shemp went on to appear in dozens of short and feature films, including playing boxing manager Knobby Walsh in the popular Joe Palooka series. In 1937, Shemp packed up his family and moved to the West Coast where his brother Moe and Larry Fine, along with little brother Curly, who had replaced him in the Stooges, had been living since 1932. Shemp did well in Hollywood, appearing in some of Abbot and Costello's best films, *Buck Privates*, *In the Navy*, *It Ain't Hay*, and *Hold That Ghost*.

Shemp later appeared as bartender Joe Guelpeas in W. C. Fields' blockbuster *The Bank Dick*. Shemp acted in *Another Thin Man*, the third of the popular Thin Man sequels, starring William Powell and Myrna Loy, and he had a role in the John Wayne and Randolph Scott vehicle *Pittsburgh*.

Shemp Howard was a successful character actor, which is surprising because during this time he suffered from major phobias that included the fear of water, flying, automobiles, heights, dogs, and large animals. He was so terrified of dogs, even though he always owned one himself, that he would howl in fear if an odd dog walked up to him. Whenever he walked around his posh Toluca Lake neighborhood, he would carry a stick with him in case of the unlikely event that he would meet a wild dog. His family always found that hilarious; Shemp was a gentle man who would never kill a fly, let alone swing a stick at a dog. It was more likely that Shemp would have fainted if a stray dog would have run up to him.

Shemp's phobias were always dealt with cleverly when he was on the studio set. During the filming of the short *Hold That Lion!*, Shemp was supposed to be in a scene with a full-grown, but elderly and drugged, lion. Shemp had a fit and refused to do the scene with the beast. Director Charles Barton had his stagehands place a thick pane of plate glass between Shemp and the lion. Still uneasy, Shemp did the scene.

During the filming of *African Screams*, Shemp and future Stooge Joe Besser had to do a scene on a raft. After being carried through the knee-deep water to the raft, Shemp clung onto Besser, terrified that he'd fall into the water. After the scene was finished, Besser jumped off and left Shemp clinging to the prop. The crew broke for lunch, leaving Shemp screaming for help, much to the amusement of the cast and crew.

Shemp's fear of cars was legendary. When traveling, he would usually lie on the backseat with a blanket over his head. If riding in the front, he would pretend he was holding an invisible steering wheel, with his foot stomping on an imaginary brake.

When little brother Curly suffered a stroke in 1946, Shemp agreed to rejoin the Stooges until Curly recovered. Curly never recovered and Shemp reluctantly stayed with the Stooges out of obligation to his brother Moe. There was no way that anyone could replace the beloved man-boy, so Shemp added his own character to the Stooges—the laid-back, female-chasing, well-meaning moron. He ended up acting in seventy-three Three Stooges shorts.

Even though Shemp despised violence, one of his favorite pastimes was attending boxing matches. Shemp would stand ringside, acting out the fight in his own unmistakable way to the cheers of the spectators. It was after attending a fight on November 22, 1955, that Shemp Howard suffered a massive heart attack in the backseat of a taxicab.

Despite his film legacy, which includes a who's who of comedic actors like John Barrymore, Marlene Dietrich, Carole Landis, Lloyd Noland, Rudy Vallee, Jack Haley, Bert Lahr, Lupe Velez, Lon Chaney Jr., Broderick Crawford, and Edgar Bergen and Charlie McCarthy, Shemp Howard will always be remembered as a Stooge.

# Chapter 20

# Nature Boy

## eden ahbez—Los Angeles

Quite possibly the first hippie in California, eden ahbez, better known as Nature Boy, was born on April 15, 1908, in Brooklyn, New York, to a Jewish family, but according to ahbez, he was adopted by a family from Kansas when he was nine years old. He moved to Los Angeles in the early 1940s, where he hung out at the raw-food restaurant and health-food store Eutropheon, on Laurel Canyon Boulevard.

First opened in 1917, Eutropheon was the place to be for free-thinking souls in Los Angeles, and it attracted an almost cult-like following. In addition to catering to health food fanatics, it was a trendy place where the Hollywood scene could relax and eat. Many of the employees and regulars grew their hair long, wore beards, and were tagged Nature Boys. They slept in the canyons and traveled to Northern California just to pick and eat figs.

Ahbez's given name was George Aberle, but he started going by eden ahbez around the time he arrived in Los Angeles. He used lowercase letters because he believed only God was worthy of capital letters. He wore white robes and lived for a time under the first L in the Hollywood sign with his wife, Anna Jacobsen. Ahbez studied Asian shamans and could be found on Hollywood street corners giving lectures about mysticism to anyone who would listen.

The couple's unusual lifestyle, especially for the 1940s, drew too much attention, so they stayed in the hills surrounding Los Angeles, most often living in the 4,210-acre Griffith Park, even after the couple had a son. The family traveled on bicycles, and their possessions consisted of a juicer and sleeping bags.

In 1947, ahbez approached Nat King Cole's manager with a song that he had written, called "Nature Boy." Cole liked the song and wanted to record it, but nobody knew where to find ahbez. Legend has it that he was found living at the foot of the Hollywood sign. Whatever the case, the manager's agents eventually did find ahbez and, even though the song rights had been given away to his various friends, a deal was made and the song was recorded.

The song was No. 1 on the charts for eight weeks in 1948, and the media had a field day with the fit and tanned long-haired man. The nation was just starting to heal after World War II, and a character like ahbez was a nice, easy news story during a time when it looked as if war with the Soviet Union was imminent. He appeared in *Time*, *Newsweek*, and *Life* magazines in the same week.

"Nature Boy" rose again in the charts later in 1948, with Frank Sinatra singing the vocals. Even though ahbez collected substantial royalties from the hit song, he and his family continued to live in the wild, riding bicycles and eating raw food. He continued to write for and sell songs to Cole, as well as to singers Eartha Kitt and Frankie Laine, but only Sam Cook's version of "Lonely Island" cracked the Top 40. But money and possessions didn't matter to ahbez.

Herman Yablokoff, a Yiddish composer, filed a lawsuit against ahbez, claiming that "Nature Boy" had the same melody as his song, "*Shvayg mayn harts*" or, in English, "Be Still My Heart." Ahbez claimed that the melody came to him in the mountains, yet he settled with Yablokoff for a substantial amount of money. Ahbez's deeply held spiritual beliefs wouldn't allow him to fight Yablokoff in court.

In 1961, Bobby Darin's recording of "Nature Boy" peaked at No. 31 on the Billboard charts. Eventually, the song would be covered by more than forty musicians, from jazz instrumentals by Miles Davis and the dazzling Sun Ra to outright laughable versions by actor Leonard Nimoy and British crooner Engelbert Humperdinck.

Ahbez continued creating music, releasing records sporadically, and he found many like-minded people once the hippie movement started in Los Angeles. He hung out with Brian Wilson during his infamous *Smile* recordings, and English pop star Donovan searched for him, eventually finding him in the desert, where they connected spiritually.

Ahbez continued to live out in the open his entire life. At the age of 86, he was hit by a car, dying from his injuries on March 4, 1995.

# Chapter 21

# Rocket Scientist

## Marvel "Jack" Parsons—Pasadena

Marvel Whiteside Parsons was born into a wealthy Pasadena family on October 2, 1914. An only child, Jack, as he was known, was surrounded by attentive servants in the family's huge Craftsman-style home at 537 Orange Grove Avenue that his grandfather, Walter Whiteside, had built. His neighbors included chewing gum magnate William Wrigley, beer baron Adolphus Busch, and the widow of assassinated president James A. Garfield. His mother, Ruth, was a patron of the embryonic Los Angeles art scene, and it was not unusual for world-class musicians and opera singers to give private performances at the twenty-room Whiteside manor.

At a young age, Jack was abandoned by his adulterous father and raised by his doting mother and aging grandparents. Home schooled until the age of twelve, Jack, a spoiled, solitary child, spent most of his time reading. He devoured books about Norse and Greek gods and King Arthur, as well as books written by science fiction pioneer Jules Verne. Jack religiously bought all of the science fiction pulp magazines, which fueled his imagination and interest in the possibility of space flight.

A limousine brought Jack to Washington Junior High School every day. His polite and proper manner did not win him friends at school, and he was often picked on for his fancy clothing and long hair. But all of that changed when Jack met Edward Foreman, two years his senior.

Foreman's family had earlier moved to Pasadena from Missouri, where they had been farmers. While not poor—Foreman's father was an electrical engineer—they were the underclass in prosperous Pasadena. Ed was tall, handsome, and streetwise, everything Jack was not. The two hit it off right away and remained friends for the rest of their lives. Foreman protected his new friend and clued him in on getting along in the real world. Together they pursued their mutual interest in science fiction and rocketry. With Jack's money and Ed's father's engineering skills, the two young men had everything they needed to pursue their flights of fancy. They started building rockets out of black powder and balsa wood tubes. As they experimented, the boys started adding fins and nose cones to their rockets, which they would launch in nearby Arroyo Seco.

In 1929, Walter Whiteside sent his family to Europe for a working vacation to buy antiques for the new home that he was having built at 285 North San Rafael Avenue. It was the only time Jack traveled outside of the United States.

Finishing up their high school classes through alternative means, the inseparable Jack and Ed continued sending their rockets into the atmosphere. Many of their launches exploded on liftoff, creating concussions that would rattle windows all over Pasadena.

The Great Depression hurt the Whiteside family, as it did most families in America, and when the old man died in 1931, Jack took a job at the Hercules Powder Factory. His knowledge about explosives led him to better positions within the company and made it easier for him to steal the ammonium nitrate, nitroglycerine, and gelatin that he needed for his and Foreman's rocket experiments.

While Parsons worked at the Hercules Powder Plant in Pinole, near San Francisco, Foreman began work as a metal apprentice at the Los Angeles Hercules plant. Both of the young men started thinking in terms of creating an engine for their rockets that would condense the thrust and allow for better control. They started building their rockets out of metal, but soon realized they needed help, as there is a lot of math involved in rocketry. They found what they needed at the nearby California Institute of Technology where, despite their lack of academic training, they joined the Guggenheim Aeronautical Laboratory and worked under Frank Malina and Theodore von Kármán. Dubbed the Suicide Squad for its daring launches, the team started making real progress with the use of solid-fuel rockets.

In 1942, Parsons devised a mixture of asphalt and potassium perchlorate, basically ushering in the jet age with this development. Using

Parsons' new formula, the team developed Jet-fuel Assisted Take Off (JATO) rockets to help lift heavy aircraft into the air. The United States government took immediate interest in JATO, and the Suicide Squad saw itself funded with more money than it could ever imagine. The project became the now world-famous Jet Propulsion Laboratory. The project group went on to form Aerojet, to manufacture rockets, missiles, and JATOs for the United States military.

Parsons' life wasn't all rocket science, as he had grown into a handsome and athletic man and had moved into his grandfather's old home at 1003 South Orange Avenue. It was a very good place in which to throw parties. Parsons and his wife, Helen Northrup, married since 1935, were followers of British occultist Aleister Crowley, and they led the Pasadena branch of Crowley's magical order, *Ordo Templi Orientis*. The couple held services at the mansion, and the Black Masses attracted the Hollywood party crowd, which thought that the mock rituals, usually involving naked women, were a hoot. Parsons, who had his first psychic experience as a boy, seriously believed in Crowley's dog and pony show and forwarded him the tithe collected from the congregation. The destitute Crowley welcomed the money, but thought that the Pasadena chapter was not following his teachings correctly. Crowley wanted Parsons to replace its current head occultist, Wilfred Smith. Crowley also wanted Parsons to keep an eye on another follower, science fiction author and future founder of the Church of Scientology, L. Ron Hubbard.

Helen's half-sister, Sara Northrup, moved into the mansion when she was seventeen, and a few years later became a serious student of *Ordo Templi Orientis*. The friction created by the femme fatale caused nothing but problems for the elite of the cult, and soon the church turned into a soap opera. Jack started an affair with Sara, and Helen ran off with Smith. Sara ended up dumping Jack for Hubbard, who also took twenty thousand dollars of Parsons' money, which he was supposed to invest in surplus ships.

On the business end of Parsons' life, things were not much better. He was forced out of Aerojet as an active partner. Some of the partners were never comfortable with the brilliant man who had only attended a few semesters of college, and the United States government was not happy that the genius behind rocket-powered flight was not only a political leftist, but also a full-fledged follower of Crowley, who was once described as the most evil man in the world. In 1944, the General Tire and Rubber

Company bought fifty-one percent of Aerojet stock. Parsons sold his interest and lived somewhat comfortably, but had he hung onto the stock, he eventually would have been worth millions of dollars.

Parsons lived a relaxed life at 1003 South Orange Avenue. He sporadically worked as a consultant for explosives companies and tinkered with fireworks and rockets through his own company, Vulcan Powder Corporation. He rented out rooms in his twenty-room home to a variety of scientists and misfits. When he needed to rent a room to make ends meet, he placed an ad in the paper that read "only bohemians, artists, musicians, atheists, anarchists, or other exotic types need apply." The parties continued, as did the Crowleyan occult ceremonies.

With the Cold War between the United States and Russia booming, the FBI, which had been keeping a file on Parsons' shenanigans, pulled his security clearance. He was unable to work for any company that held government contracts. To make matters worse, his new wife, Candy, left him.

Parsons started working several menial jobs, even pumping gasoline on the weekends. His friend Ed Foreman was not doing much better. Eventually, Parsons got his security clearance back and obtained employment with Hughes Aircraft. He also started to negotiate with Israel to take over its fledgling rocket program. Caught by the FBI, Parsons was investigated for espionage. Interviewing witnesses of, and participants in, the Black Masses held at Parsons' house unleashed buckets of juicy gossip, which flew around the Los Angeles area. Accusations of drug use and ritual sex sold magazines. Parsons' house was bugged and he was followed by agents.

Candy and Jack reconciled and leased the coach house at 1071 South Orange Grove. The house was the only original building standing on the property, which was once home to the Cruikshank estate. The bottom floor of the house had been converted into a laundry room/laboratory, where Parsons brewed absinthe and stored his explosives. Jack and Candy hosted many parties, which attracted artists, writers, and musicians of all kinds. Jazz great Charlie Parker is said to have attended these fêtes, at which bongos were played into the early morning hours.

With all of the war and science fiction films being made, Parsons found his skills valuable to the film industry. On June 17, 1952, Parsons received a rush order from a Hollywood special effects company to make small explosives that mimicked a body being shot. Being in a hurry because he and Candy had planned a Mexican vacation for the next day, Jack found himself the victim of his own innovation when something went horribly wrong in his backyard lab and two almost simultaneous explosions shook Pasadena at 5:08 p.m. Jack Parsons died from his injuries shortly after arriving at the hospital. He was thirty-seven years old.

When the fire department arrived, they were so stunned by the amount of volatile chemicals that had not exploded that they called the army's Fifty-Eighth Ordinance Disposal Unit to deal with the removal.

Jack's mother, Ruth, was so shocked by her son's death that she followed him four hours later with an overdose of barbiturates.

# Chapter 22

# Friday on His Mind

## Jack Webb—Los Angeles

Born to a mother who filed divorce papers on his father before he was born, Jack Webb, the actor, director, writer, and producer, was born into poverty in 1920s Los Angeles. A sickly child, Webb lived with his mother and grandmother, both of whom worked menial jobs, often at night. Jack dove into reading anything he could get his hands on, and he could often be seen going through garbage cans behind his Bunker Hill apartment for reading material. A jazz enthusiast neighbor introduced young Webb to jazz music by giving him a Bix Beiderbecke record. It started his lifelong love of the music.

As a student at Belmont High School, Webb emceed variety shows, stealing his jokes from comedians he had heard on the radio. He was so popular that he was elected class president. After high school, Webb received a scholarship to Chouinard Art Institute, but he eventually had to drop out of school to help support his ailing mother and grandmother.

World War II found Webb working in an armory plant and landing bit parts in radio dramas. Tired of waiting for his draft number to come up, he joined the Army Air Corps, washed

### Jack Webb's Old Neighborhood

Bunker Hill, the neighborhood where Jack Webb grew up, was lowered and cleared during the 1950s for urban renewal. The site is now LA's modern downtown.

washed out as a pilot, and ended up typing correspondence at an air base in Del Rio, Texas. With his mother and grandmother ailing, Webb applied for and received a dependency discharge. As the war exploded throughout the world, the shortage of men in the workforce increased. Webb landed a position at KGO radio in San Francisco, using his time there to learn as much as he could about radio production. He would practice voice modulation for hours in front of a dead microphone and talk shop with the engineers. After several weeks, Webb was promoted to voice announcer, and eventually he hosted an early morning jazz program called *The Coffee Club*.

With his energy, self-confidence, and fervent desire for perfection, Webb soon found himself in the position of lead actor in the radio program *Pat Novak for Hire*. Webb, who had already worked as a contributing writer on the program, was told by co-writer Richard Breen not to ham it up but to underplay Novak. Webb took this suggestion to the extreme and played the private detective as the ultimate hard-boiled wise guy, one who mouthed off to both cops and criminals. Even though the story line was pretty much the same each week, the show attained a loyal following in the San Francisco Bay Area.

Breen got a film offer in Hollywood that coincidentally happened just after he had had an argument with KGO's management. Webb, who roomed with Breen, headed to Los Angeles with him.

Webb and Breen were signed by the Mutual Network to create and act in new radio programs. Radio was a fading medium by 1947, but Webb kept busy, acting in a half-dozen radio programs. One of his shows, *Johnny Madero*, provided Webb with enough financial security to marry his girlfriend, actress and singer Julie London.

Being a freelancer, Webb was used to contributing creative ideas, but his big mouth and confident manner turned off directors and producers. Consequently, Webb had a hard time finding work. His agent got him small roles in radio and film, including a minor part as William Holden's jazz-loving friend in *Sunset Boulevard* and roles in the noir classics *Dark City* and *He Walked by Night*. Taking a page from the latter role, Webb developed a police show for radio, based on true stories from the Los Angeles Police Department files.

*Dragnet* first aired on June 3, 1949. Using clipped, clever, and straightforward dialog, Webb, as Sergeant Joe Friday, joined with his partner to solve uniquely Los Angeles crimes for three hundred and eighteen episodes. In late 1951, *Dragnet* appeared on NBC as a television show and, until the radio program was canceled in 1955, two different versions of *Dragnet* were produced in separate media.

The 1951 television version of *Dragnet* eclipsed the radio program and became a big hit with viewers. After a series of sidekicks, Ben Alexander settled in as Officer Frank Smith for the duration of the series. Webb, a stickler for detail, had a representative of the Los Angeles Police Department on the set for accuracy, as he wanted to portray police in a positive light, far removed from the corrupt cops in his earlier work. The quick editing and close-ups of the actors worked perfectly on the small screen.

Webb filmed everything as quickly and as cheaply as possible. His greatest breakthrough in low-quality TV production came when he met Stanley Meyer, who owned the patent on the TelePrompTer. The TelePrompTer is an electronic screen that displays an actor's lines and was designed to replace cue cards. Webb discovered that if actors read their lines directly from the TelePrompTer without rehearsing, there was virtually no difference in their performances. With all of the close-ups used in *Dragnet*, the TelePrompTer was the perfect tool for the program. Webb saved money by not rehearsing his actors, became an investor in the TelePrompTer, and hired Meyer to run his company, Mark VII Productions.

*Dragnet* was on the air for two hundred and seventy-six episodes, until 1959. It was one of the first network television programs to be syndicated. Lunch boxes, toy guns, and cigarettes were all merchandised with the *Dragnet* logo. Webb even released an album of love songs, which he spoke rather than sang.

Webb was the producer and director of *Dragnet*, and he ran the set like an army camp. There was no pampering of the actors, and everyone was treated fairly, as long as no one screwed up a scene.

Always on the lookout for film opportunities, Webb was able to finagle a multi-film deal after the success of *Dragnet*. He directed and starred in *The D.I.*— the title is military terminology for a drill instructor. Webb yelled so much in the movie that his once-smooth baritone turned into a raspy croak. On the plus side, he liked his military crew cut so much that he adopted it for the rest of his life.

Webb also directed and starred in *Pete Kelly's Blues*, which in 2009 was named by the British film magazine *Empire* as "the thirteenth best gangster film you've never seen." The cast included Janet Leigh, Peggy Lee, Ella Fitzgerald, Lee Marvin, and a very young Jayne Mansfield. Webb had high hopes for his jazz-heavy drama, but it did poorly at the box office. Peggy Lee was nominated for Best Supporting Actress, and the sound track was nominated for a Grammy, but Webb's careless comments about show business and the people who run it again put him out of favor with the studio heads. Webb was the perfect example of biting the hand that feeds you.

Original episodes of *Dragnet* went off the air in 1959, and Webb found himself without work. He was on his third marriage and had to pay child support for the two daughters he had with London, who had divorced him in 1954. He feared the poverty he grew up in, and constantly floated pilots and scripts to networks and studios, but they had had enough of the mouthy man whose ego was bigger than his talent. Many Hollywood insiders felt that, had Webb not always filmed on the fast and cheap and actually taken some time with his projects, he could have been the equal of Orson Welles and John Ford.

In 1963, Webb took over as executive producer of the smash hit *77 Sunset Strip*. He fired everyone but its main star, Efrem Zimbalist, Jr. The show sank to the bottom of the ratings and was cancelled later that year.

In 1966, much to Webb's dismay, there was interest in a new *Dragnet*. Webb wanted to move on from the show, but he was on wife number three and had to pay alimony and child support, and he couldn't afford to turn down the offer.

Webb hired actor Harry Morgan to play his partner, Bill Gannon. Having witnessed Webb's tirades on the set, Morgan quickly learned to let Webb do things his own way. The two characters wore the same suits in every episode so that they could simultaneously shoot different episodes while on the same set. It made things simple when they had to reshoot a scene. Everything was read off of the TelePrompTer. When close-ups were shot, the actors sat in chairs and read their lines. This caused problems with many of the actors, who were used to actually acting. If an actor embellished his lines, Webb would yell "Cut!," and then tell the actor, "That was great! You could win the Academy Award with that performance. But that isn't how we do things on *Dragnet*. Now just read the goddamn lines." Many actors couldn't adjust to Webb's way of performing, and they were either fired on the spot or never asked back. The actors who played the game that Webb wanted to play were rewarded with steady work on the show.

Webb did not tolerate any horsing around on the set. He would spend twenty minutes berating a grip or soundman for the slightest thing, screaming about how much money was wasted because of a mistake. But Webb was also quick to laugh at himself. Once you got used to the way Webb wanted things done, he was easy to get along with.

It was expected of Webb's employees that they would hang out with him after the day was over to drink scotch and eat steaks at the Cock and Bull Restaurant on Sunset Boulevard until the early hours of the morning. Many Mark VII employees' marriages broke up because of the drunken late nights with Webb. Many of those nights ended up at his apartment across the street, where Webb would play DJ, spinning his jazz records through the latest audio equipment. He had one of the largest jazz record collections in the world.

*Dragnet* tackled such social problems of the day as drug addiction, child abuse, and racial inequality. The show's final scenes always ended with what Webb called "the goddamn Jesus speech," where he would tell the criminal exactly what he thought before he made his arrest. Webb hated doing *Dragnet* and the cut-and-paste production showed his attitude. In another life, Webb would have made a fine factory manager.

By 1970, *Dragnet* was finished. Webb was more interested in producing other shows for Mark VII, with *Adam-12* and *Emergency* being his biggest hits.

Jack Webb died of a massive heart attack in his apartment on December 23, 1982. The Los Angeles Police Department flew its flags at half-staff that day, and a week later the department gave Webb an official memorial service, the first ever given to a civilian. Joe Friday's badge number, 714, was retired from service.

# Chapter 23

## Genius in Angora

### Ed Wood—Los Angeles

The entertainment world has never had a shortage of individuals whose ambition is greater than their talent, but few have been as well documented as writer, director, producer, and actor Ed Wood, Jr.

Born in Poughkeepsie, New York, Ed Jr. saw Bela Lugosi in the movie *Dracula* when he was seven years old and was forever hooked on scary movies. Young Ed received his first movie camera for his eleventh birthday, and he started shooting movies in his backyard with his friends and classmates.

After graduating from high school, Wood quit his job as a movie usher and joined the United States Marine Corps at the start of World War II. He fought in the bloody Battle of Tarawa, coming in on the second wave of amphibious landing craft. The first wave had been almost entirely wiped out. Wood saw his share of combat, and in one vicious skirmish engaged in hand-to-hand combat, got bayoneted, and lost his front teeth to a Japanese rifle butt. Wood killed the soldier in his foxhole. After he recovered from his wounds, he was transferred to underwater reconnaissance and sabotage. What the military brass didn't know was that their highly decorated Marine always wore ladies' undergarments.

After the war, Wood attended college for a short time and then found himself working with a traveling circus. Fascinated by the carnies and freaks, Ed took any job that was open, including the half-man-half-woman and the geek. A circus geek is one of the lowest entrées into show business, yet Wood's desire to be in the entertainment world was so strong that he would bite the heads off of live rats in front of a paying crowd. He felt at home with the circus people, who aren't exactly known for being socially discriminating.

Wood ended up in Hollywood in 1947 with optimism in his step, and soon found himself performing in local plays and appearing as an extra in movies. His buoyant personality and big talk attracted a group of actors, some green, others on the downslide of their careers. Despite his obsession with angora sweaters and penchant for wearing women's clothing, Ed had a thing for the ladies, and the ladies found him hard to resist. Frequenting Hollywood hot spots like the Brown Derby and Ciro's, where he rubbed elbows with real movie stars, Wood started to collect an entourage of freaks, weirdos, and even some real actors, like John Agar, John Carradine, and Kenn Duncan.

In 1951, Wood joined the Screen Actors Guild and began directing a television drama called *The Sun Was Setting*, which he also wrote. He met his idol, Bela Lugosi, and started a friendship with the Hungarian-born actor that would last until Lugosi's death. Lugosi, once the most popular box office draw in America, was a morphine addict who became a pariah in the film world. Also around this time, Wood married his first wife, but the marriage was short-lived. She could not handle her husband's fetish for wearing women's clothing, and she kicked Wood out on their wedding night.

With two directing credits on his résumé, and Bela Lugosi as a name to drop to investors, Wood found writer, actor, and producer George Weiss to produce his first film, *Glen or Glenda*. Weiss sold the film to distributors before a single line was written.

*Glen or Glenda* was planned as an exploitation film from the start. Making the headlines of newspapers all over the world in 1952 was World War II veteran George Jorgensen, who underwent the first sex reassignment surgery and became Christine Jorgensen.

The movie starred a drug-addicted Bela Lugosi as the scientist, Lyle Talbot, and Wood's current beautiful and blonde girlfriend Dolores Fuller. Ed Wood played Glen and Glenda. Fuller, who would make *Jailbait* and *Bride of the Monster* with Wood, went on to become a successful songwriter, penning songs for Elvis Presley, Shelley Fabares, and Nat King Cole.

*Glen or Glenda* is a bizarre mix of documentary style exploitation, with a mad scientist (Lugosi) in his laboratory playing God; Glen, a tormented man who wishes he were female (Wood); Glen's confused girlfriend (Fuller); and a police detective (Talbot) who goes to a doctor (Timothy Farrell, who was an L.A. County court bailiff) to get some understanding about a dead transvestite case he is working on. Glen tries to find a happy balance in his tormented life and does so toward the end of the film, when Fuller's character enthusiastically removes her angora sweater and hands it to Glen, who beams with happiness. The film is filled with hammy acting and bad direction, interspersed with scenes of mild bondage and stock footage of stampeding buffalo that come out of nowhere. While *Glen or Glenda* was sold as an exploitation film to be shown at drive-ins and second-rate theaters, it did have a positive message about cross-dressing and alternative lifestyles that most of the other exploitation flicks of that era did not have.

Wood next directed and filmed *Jailbait*, an interesting crime film with a great plot twist. *Jailbait* is technically Wood's best film, but the cheap sets and bad acting overpower the story, making it an entertainingly laughable film. Wood always worked on the cheap and rarely shot more than one take on any of his films. Wood let his actors improvise, but, unfortunately, none of his actors were any good at improvising. Wood had zero business sense, paying his actors and technicians in crumpled bills and promising more percentage of the profits than was mathematically possible. Production started or stopped depending on how long the money lasted. This was the business plan Wood used throughout his career.

During the next four years, Wood worked on an astonishing seven film projects, as either writer or director. They offered the same low-budget exploitation fare, yet Wood was living his dream. His stable of stars included Lugosi, Fuller, Duke Moore, Conrad Brooks, and former Swedish wrestler Tor Johnson. The films had ingenious titles, like *Bride of the Monster*, *The Violent Years*, *The Astounding She-Monster*, *Final Curtain*, *The Night the Banshee Cried*, *The Bride and the Beast*, and *Night of the Ghoul*. Most of these films were billed under different names, depending on the region and the distributor.

Although Wood's films seemed to be slapped together without much forethought, there was always a script of some kind, even if Wood had written it in a mere four hours. His scripts always had an outrageous quality to them, whether it was a gang of teenage juvenile delinquent girls raping a man off camera or a woman falling in love with her husband's pet gorilla.

Wood was able to convince his landlord, a Baptist minister, to financially back his greatest feature, *Plan 9 from Outer Space*. The Baptist Church of Beverly Hills wanted to make religious films, and church officers came to the conclusion that they could put money into a quickie exploitation film and make a fast buck to finance their main projects. The church insisted that, before any money was given to Wood, his entire entourage had to be baptized. This being the Baptist Church of Beverly Hills, the ceremony took place in a swimming pool.

Using two scenes of Bela Lugosi shortly before he died in 1955, Wood was able to staple together what is generally accepted as the worst film ever made. Originally called *Grave Robbers from Outer Space*, its title was changed by its distributor, Hal Roach Distributing Corporation, to the more spectacular-sounding *Plan 9 from Outer Space*.

The movie starred former wrestler Tor Johnson; TV horror hostess Maila Nurmi, known as Vampira; washed-up movie stars Tom Keene and Lyle Talbot; San Francisco radio announcer Dudley Manlove; psychic-to-the-stars, The Amazing Criswell, as the narrator; and child molester and trust-fund homosexual John "Bunny" Breckinridge as the most effeminate alien leader in film history. The movie has shockingly bad dialog, laughable special effects, and props that fall over. Random stock footage, along with lighting and continuity problems, intertwined with bad acting to help the movie through its slow parts, but it is not without purposeful humor. The message of the film is that humans are stupid and should quit building weapons of mass destruction.

Production on *Plan 9 from Outer Space* was the usual on-again, off-again method that Wood had used throughout his career, and he again paid his actors and crew in crumpled bills and IOUs. Wood was drunk throughout the filming and rarely shot more than one take of each scene. The film played drive-ins and small towns for four years after it was made.

Wood began the downward spiral that most alcoholics tumble down after years of late nights and rowdy parties. The notorious skirt-wearing, skirt-chasing Ed Wood tied the knot with Kathy O'Hara Everett, a foul-mouthed drunk from Canada. Ed and Kathy would get drunk and argue for hours, often resulting in physical fights.

The couple lived in a seedy apartment at Yucca and Cahuenga, which in the 1970s was one of the most dangerous neighborhoods in Hollywood. As Wood got older and more alcoholic, he tended to stay in drag all of the time, which made him an easy target for the neighborhood's criminal element. Wood made more movies, but they got in the way of his drinking; to pay the rent, he made pornographic film loops and wrote pulp fiction books for a hundred dollars a pop. Wood knocked out dozens of sensational sex-filled books for the reading public. He could sit in front of a blaring television, cigarette in mouth, whiskey next to him, Kathy screaming at him, and write one hundred pages in a day. There are at least fifty pulp fiction books credited to Ed Wood, with tantalizing titles like *Orgy of the Dead*, *It Takes One to Know One*, *Death of a Transvestite*, *Night Time Lez*, *To Make a Homo*, and *Death of a Transvestite Hooker*.

In December 1978, the Woods were evicted from their apartment by the Los Angeles Sheriff's Department. They were allowed to take only one suitcase apiece with them, and, thus, Wood lost his lifetime collection of film scripts, negatives, manuscripts, and film. The items were thrown into a dumpster behind the building. Desperate, and with few friends left, the couple moved in with Ed's old friend, Peter Coe, at 5635 Laurel Canyon Boulevard.

On December 10, 1978, Wood went upstairs into Coe's bedroom to get away from his nagging, drunken wife. He suffered a heart attack and called and pleaded for Kathy to come to him. She thought that Ed was just trying to get attention, and she ignored him. Only after he had stopped calling for her, did she go upstairs to see what he wanted. Ed Wood was dead at age fifty-four.

There is no doubt that Ed Wood was a talented man, but his vices got the best of him. Had he lived a few more years, he would have enjoyed the limelight again as his films grew in popularity with the hipster crowd and film buffs, who loved Wood's artistic view, warts and all.

# Chapter 24

## The Not-So-Little Rascal

### Carl Switzer—Los Angeles

Carl Switzer and his older brother, Harold, were popular entertainers in the little town of Paris, Illinois, where they lived. They sang and danced, performed comedy skits, and engaged in general buffoonery whenever they got the chance.

In 1934, while on a trip to visit relatives in Los Angeles, the family took a tour of the Hal Roach Studios, where the popular *Our Gang* shorts were filmed. While in the Our Gang Café, the studio's cafeteria, six-year-old Carl and eight-year-old Harold broke into one of their musical skits. Carl hammed it up with his comical, off-key singing and exaggerated, angelic facial expressions, and Hal Roach signed them on the spot.

Carl was given a giant cowlick in his hair and a new name, Alfalfa. He quickly became a favorite of the series, the mischievous country bumpkin. Even though he sang horribly, he was usually scripted to sing one song, much to the dismay of the adults in the series. Harold resigned himself to being a background actor.

Switzer was aware of his popularity with his audience and pushed as many of the cast's and crew's buttons as possible. He was a bully and played dangerous pranks on his fellow actors that sometimes required stitches. Switzer once urinated on some stage lighting, causing the bulbs to explode when they were turned on. Production was stopped as a room-clearing odor filled the stage. The expensive bulbs had to be replaced. Switzer often refused to participate in his studies at the studio school, and he would often hold up filming over a temper tantrum.

The *Our Gang* series wrapped up in 1940, and Switzer, at the age of twelve, found that maintaining an acting career in Hollywood wasn't as easy as starting one. His reputation as an egotistical prankster did not endear him to the studio bosses. Switzer obtained small parts in a dozen movies before he found himself basically unemployable in the industry.

Alfie, as he was known to his few friends, grew up to be a gloomy, bitter young man. He was angry that his film career seemed to be over before he could even get a driver's license, so he drank and moped. He was a braggart, telling outrageous stories that nobody believed or cared about.

In 1957, Switzer moved to Kansas and married a rich farmer's daughter. The marriage lasted four months and resulted in a son, but Switzer soon found himself back in California. He managed to find occasional work in television and films, but he usually worked as a bartender and hunting guide.

While Alfie and the other actors in the *Our Gang* series were basically living hand-to-mouth, *Our Gang* was rechristened *The Little Rascals* and sold to television. It raked in millions of dollars, yet none of the former castmates received a penny.

Alfie was arrested in Sequoia National Park for illegally cutting down trees. He was so desperate for money that he was poaching small evergreens to sell as Christmas trees back in Los Angeles. He was fined two hundred and fifty dollars and given probation, but time was running out for the reckless, washed-up actor.

In February 4, 1958, Switzer was shot while getting into his car in Studio City. It was only a flesh wound, but Eugene Earl Butler was charged with "suspicion of assault with intent to murder." Switzer was dating Butler's ex-wife, Susan.

Switzer borrowed a hunting dog from his friend and sometime business partner, Moses "Bud" Stilz, but Alfie somehow lost the valuable dog. After offering a fifty-dollar reward, Switzer was contacted by the man who found it. The man met Alfie at the bar where he worked, and Alfie paid him the reward. Alfie ended up paying the man's fifteen dollar bar tab, too.

A few nights later, on January 21, 1959, Alfie, in a drunken stupor, decided that Stilz owed him the reward money. With his friend, Jack Piott, Alfie drove to where Stilz was staying in Mission Hills. Stilz's girlfriend and future wife, Rita Corrigan, the former wife of stuntman Crash Corrigan, answered the door.

There are always a couple of different sides to every violent action, but this is the official version of what happened next: Switzer flashed a fake police badge and demanded the money from Stiltz, an argument erupted, and Switzer hit Stilz over the head with a glass-domed clock. Bruised and bloody, Stilz grabbed a pistol from his dresser draw and Alfie lunged for it; they fell to the floor and wrestled. The gun went off, the bullet hitting the ceiling. Alfie got the gun, but Stiltz grappled it back and shot Switzer in the stomach as Switzer was pulling out a knife. Carl Switzer died at a nearby hospital.

Stilz was exonerated from any charges because he had clearly acted in self-defense. Rita Corrigan and her three children, as well as Switzer's friend, Jack Piott, all witnessed the attack by the drunken, fallen star.

A few years later, Carl's brother Harold committed suicide after murdering a business partner. Showbiz was not good to the Switzer boys.

# Chapter 25

## 20th Century Nostradamus

### Jerome King Criswell—Los Angeles

*Greetings, my friend. We are all interested in the future, for that is where you and I are going to spend the rest of our lives. And, remember, my friend, future events such as these will affect you in the future. You are interested in the unknown, the mysterious, the unexplainable. That is why you are here. And, now, for the first time, we are bringing to you the full story of what happened on that fateful day. We are giving you all the evidence, based only on the secret testimonies of the miserable souls who survived this terrifying ordeal. The incidents, the places, my friend, we cannot keep this a secret any longer. Let us punish the guilty. Let us reward the innocent. My friend, can your heart stand the shocking facts about grave robbers from outer space?*

Any fan of bad cinema will instantly recognize the above drivel as the handiwork of The Amazing Criswell in the film, *Plan 9 from Outer Space*. Criswell appeared in the film as a favor to his good friend, Ed Wood, who was scraping by to get his sixth film produced.

Born as Jeron Charles Criswell King or Jerome Criswell Konig on August 18, 1907, in Princeton, Indiana, to a family of morticians, Criswell claimed to have been raised in the family's funeral home. He sought refuge from his parent's bickering by hiding in the casket storeroom, sleeping in one of the many coffins in storage, a habit that he allegedly continued throughout his life.

According to Criswell, he went to college, studied journalism, and was a radio announcer in New York City. All completely believable, as Criswell was an educated man with a great booming voice that was perfect for radio announcing. While announcing on KCOP Channel 13 in Los Angeles during the late 1940s, Criswell finished a live ad with several minutes of airtime left. Not wanting dead air, Criswell improvised some silly predictions until the slot was over. So many people called in about his predictions that Criswell bought airtime and *Criswell Predicts* was launched. The show was so popular that it was picked up by eighty-five stations nationally. By 1950, he had a syndicated newspaper column that appeared in over one hundred and fifty newspapers around the country. He also wrote a popular book in 1950, *Success without Struggle.*

Criswell was perfect for the new medium of television. He was a handsome man, with white hair and a spit curl on his forehead. He wore black tuxedos with sequined lapels, heavy makeup, and, with the help of backlighting, appeared to be authoritative as he spouted out nonsensical predictions that were as wild as they were inaccurate.

Here are a few of Criswell's predictions:

- I predict that man's exploration of space and the building of space stations will be the salvation of the human race. By 1999. there will be more than two hundred of these space stations in existence. They will house entire colonies—men, women, and children. When the earth is destroyed on August 18, 1999, these space colonists will be the only Earth-humans left in the Universe.
- I predict that perversion will flood the land, beginning in 1970. I predict a series of homosexual cities, small, compact, carefully planned areas, will soon be blatantly advertised and exist from coast to coast. These compact communities will be complete with stores, churches, bars, and restaurants that will put the olden Greeks or Romans to shame with their organized orgies. You will be able to find them near Boston, Des Moines, Columbus, Philadelphia, Washington, D.C., San Francisco, St. Louis, New Orleans, Dallas, and Miami. Much thought and planning will be expended in setting up these communities where perversion will parade shamelessly. And, all this will be within the law because the perverted will claim they have been discriminated against. The Supreme Court will rule that whatever these consenting adult males, or females, wish to do, they can!
- I predict that on February 11, 1981, there will be an abortive attempt by a foreign power to bomb the United States with atomic missiles. Most of the missiles will be destroyed by anti-missile missiles, but

several will be only driven off course and will drop on the helpless state of Vermont. The death toll on that date will exceed 50,000 persons.

- In Florida, billions of dollars will be spent to prevent the Atlantic Ocean's gradual inundation of the entire peninsula. Entire cities will be relocated, beginning in 1979.
- New York will not exist as we know it today after January 21, 1980. Shifting ocean currents and earth tremors will begin to remake the eastern coast of the United States, beginning in 1971. At first, the changes will be small, but within three years our geologists will know what is happening. As the coastline shifts, the land will sink and the ocean will pour inland. Before 1978, Long Island will be mostly underwater. Only the areas that can be protected by hastily erected dikes will escape—and they, not for long. Manhattan will become a city of canals, like Venice. Billions of dollars will be spent to save New York, but by 1980, all efforts will have failed and a new New York will rise, further inland, at a great expense.

Even a broken clock is correct twice a day, and Criswell did manage to get a few predictions right. He predicted that President John F. Kennedy would not run for reelection, and on December 31, 1965, while a guest on the *Tonight Show* with Johnny Carson, Criswell predicted that Ronald Reagan would be elected governor of California. But for the most part, Criswell merely titillated the public with his often risqué prophecies.

Criswell enjoyed the limelight and openly admitted that he had no gift for predicting the future, but as long as people paid, he did not care. Criswell always had an entourage of misfits and hangers-on, which included his wife, exotic dancer Halo Meadows, and her ever-present standard poodle, which she believed was the reincarnation of her dead cousin. Criswell and his group held court almost nightly at the ritzy Brown Derby Restaurant. He was invited to many Hollywood Hills parties, where he dazzled and amused the entertainment industry elite.

One of Criswell's best friends was comedienne/actress/writer Mae West. Despite West's reputation for being a fully liberated woman, she was an extraordinary home chef, and she would often send her chauffeur to Criswell's home to deliver her home-cooked meals. On her 1956 Decca album, *The Fabulous Mae West*, she regaled the psychic talents of her friend with the song "Criswell Predicts." Whenever West bought a new limousine, she would sell her old vehicle to Criswell for one dollar. Criswell, with one of his hangers-on acting as chauffeur, enjoyed riding around the Hollywood hotspots in his Cadillac.

Criswell was smart with his money, and he owned an unpretentious apartment building in Hollywood, where he had potluck dinners with his friends among his collection of coffins.

Criswell was good friends with Ed Wood, who looked up to Criswell for advice and support. Besides *Plan 9 from Outer Space*, Criswell also appeared in two other Ed Wood films, *Night of the Ghouls* and *Orgy of the Dead.* Allegedly, Criswell was one of the investors in *Plan 9 from Outer Space*, and owned a print that was showed in a New York City theater for over a year. Criswell earned back his investment, and more.

Throughout the sixties and seventies, Criswell kept himself in the public eye. He made numerous television appearances with Jack Parr, Mike Douglas, Merv Griffin, and on Johnny Carson's *Tonight Show*, where he still astonished audiences with his predictions. Between 1968 and 1972, Criswell published three books, *Criswell's Forbidden Predictions: Based on Nostradamus and the Tarot*; *Your Next Ten Years: Criswell Predicts*; and *Criswell Predicts from Now to the Year 2000!*

After suffering several stokes, Criswell's health deteriorated, and he died of heart failure on October 4, 1982. Nobody knows if he predicted his own death.

# Chapter 26

## A Brilliant Man

### Hermann Schultheis—Los Angeles

Hermann Schultheis was born to be a Californian. Born in Aachen, Germany, in 1900, he graduated in 1926 with a Ph.D. in mechanical and electrical engineering from the Institute of Technology at Aachen. Soon after he graduated, he moved to New York City, where he became an successful electro-acoustic design engineer working for Western Electric and Bell Laboratories and The Radio Electric Clock Companies of New York. Schultheis was instrumental in the development of the clock radio. He also designed an optical printer and a stereoscopic drum camera, and he worked on advancing light transmission and measuring equipment. In addition, he discovered a new process for restoring old paintings for the Art Conservation and Research Laboratory in New York City.

Schultheis married Ethel Wisloh on June 27, 1936, and two years later, they moved to California, after Schultheis was hired by Walt Disney Studios. The Schultheises immediately fell in love with the Southern California lifestyle. The charming and intelligent couple made friends easily and were sought-after guests for parties.

During Schultheis's three years at Disney, he researched color photography, sound recording, and advanced special effects techniques. His work was used in the Disney films *Bambi*, *Dumbo*, *Fantasia*, *Pinocchio*, and *Snow White and the Seven Dwarfs*.

During the war years, Schultheis worked for 20th Century Fox as a research and development engineer. While there, he developed electro-acoustic instruments and advanced miniature model photography.

Telefilm Studios hired Schultheis as its chief engineer in charge of technical processes and research. He designed the universal camera crane for animation, title, and model work. He was also the co-inventor of a background matte process to make live-action models appear more realistic, a process now known as a blue screen. Schultheis also did research at the California Institute of Technology, where he designed ultra-high-speed cameras and improved the technology for underwater photography. In 1949, Schultheis became the technical research librarian at Librascope, one of the first digital computer companies in the world. As a consultant, he was the go-to guy for stumped engineers.

Hermann was far from being an all-work and no-fun scientist. He was known for his great sense of humor. There are few photos of Schultheis where he is not mugging for the camera. He was also a concert-grade pianist and entertained his friends with brilliant playing.

The blond, well-built, and well-tanned Schultheis was an incessant photographer. There was nothing that Schultheis would not take a photo of: oil wells, farmer's markets, billboards, county fairs, factories, street life, ribbon cutting ceremonies, and people standing in line. Schultheis loved the ocean and took hundreds of photos—usually with beautiful girls in the frame—of Huntington, Hermosa, Venice, Malibu, and Laguna beaches. During a time when few photographers thought about ethnic minorities, Schultheis documented Japanese, Mexican, Filipino, and Chinese Los Angelinos at work and play. Schultheis had the foresight to thoroughly photograph Los Angeles' Old Chinatown before it was torn down to make way for the construction of Union Station.

Possibly because he was from the same city as the pioneer of modern architecture and the last director of the Bauhaus, Ludwig Mies van der Rohe, Schultheis had an eye for architecture and took thousands of photos of homes and businesses in Los Angeles. Thanks to Schultheis' work, over two thousand of his photographs of then-mundane and now-fascinating aspects of Los Angeles belong to the Los Angeles Public Library.

Hermann and Ethel lived in Los Feliz, and their house was a site to behold. Hermann had rigged the electrical system to automatically do as many things as possible directly from his desk. He could turn lights, radios, and the television on and off, open and close windows, and even serve drinks with the touch of a button.

His darkroom was his domain, neatly organized in stainless steel shelving, as was most of their home. Thousands of negatives, miles of microfilm, and a huge collection of photographic equipment filled the room.

The Schultheis living room was decorated in a tropical theme, accessorized with art and relics that they had picked up on their many trips to the Middle East and Central and South America. In the 1950s, Schultheis was intrigued with Guatemala and its ancient ruins. He annually hiked alone in the jungle looking for Maya artifacts and abandoned temples.

In May 1955, Schultheis took a trip alone to Guatemala to explore more ruins. He hired a pilot in Flores to take him deep into the jungle so he could explore the Mayan site of Tikal. Everyone warned him not to go alone and to hire a local guide to help, but he shrugged off the advice and flew into the one of the most isolated regions in the Western Hemisphere during the rainy season.

A few hours later, when the pilot landed to pick Schultheis up at the airstrip, the engineer was nowhere to be found. The pilot flew back the next day and still found no Schultheis. The Guatemalan military sent out a search party and after a week gave up the search to find him.

Eighteen months later, in November 1956, a chicle gum camp worker found Schultheis's remains and belongings. His body was far too decomposed to determine the cause of death.

Ethel never remarried, and after she died in 1990, Schultheis' photo collection was given to the Los Angeles County Library. While at Disney, Schultheis kept a thorough record of the work that he and his team created: thousands of drawings, photographs, film clips, graphs, sketches, and written descriptions of the techniques that were used to create the groundbreaking art of animation. The notebooks now belong to the Walt Disney Family Museum in San Francisco, where it can be seen in person and online.

# Chapter 27

# Lovable Crank

## William Frawley—Los Angeles

William Frawley will forever be known to television buffs as Fred Mertz, neighbor and landlord to Ricky and Lucy Ricardo in the pioneer television series *I Love Lucy*. His grumpy wisecracks and impeccable comic timing gave Frawley the biggest laughs every week that the show aired on CBS, from October 15, 1951, to May 6, 1957, and then again in thirteen one-hour specials until 1960. Unbeknownst to most viewers, Fred Mertz was a merely toned-down version of William Frawley, without the profanities, racist jokes, and misogyny.

Born to Mike and Mary Frawley on February 16, 1887, in the Mississippi River town of Burlington, Iowa, Bill grew up in relative prosperity. Mike Frawley was an insurance man and civic booster of Burlington who made sure that his children, John, Bill, Paul, and Mary, received a good Catholic upbringing. Mary wanted only the best for her children, which meant her kids would all get good jobs with the railroad, get married, and have children.

Bill loved sports and singing and he did both whenever he could. His smooth baritone would bring tears to the eyes of the toughest railroad workers. He had dreams of leaving Burlington and becoming a vaudevillian, going to new places and meeting interesting people.

Mike Frawley died in 1907 at age fifty, which gave Bill more leeway to pursue his dream of performing. For awhile, Frawley toiled at a boring insurance job, but managed to get himself transferred to Chicago with the intentions of going into show business. Once in Chicago, Frawley wasted no time in pursuing his aspiring entertainment career, and he appeared on stage in short order in the chorus of *The Flirting Princess.* Mary—who had incredible pull with her children, even when they were adults—soon found out that Bill had quit his insurance job to sing and dance on stage, and she sent his brother John to retrieve him. John gave Bill a letter from their mother in which she proclaimed that she would rather see him dead than watch him wreck his life as an actor. When Bill arrived back in Burlington, he took a job with the railroad. No doubt his domineering mother, who constantly threw roadblocks in front of his dreams, triggered a lifelong disdain for female relationships.

Bill and brother Paul put together a song and dance act, and they tried it out in an East Saint Louis vaudeville house. The act went over well and, after acquiring stage experience, they worked the Midwest vaudeville circuit as The Frawley Brothers, until Paul left the act to attend college, at Mary's insistence. Eventually, Paul left the Midwest for the New York City stage, where his handsome looks and good voice kept him working on Broadway for the next twenty years. Mary died in 1921, and, after attending Mary's funeral, Bill Frawley never went back to Burlington, Iowa.

Bill teamed up with pianist Franz Rath with an act called *A Man, A Piano, and a Nut*, and they landed a year-long gig at Denver's popular Rex Café. Once their contract was up in Denver, they hit the Western and Pacific Coast vaudeville circuits. One night, they could be performing for the super-rich at Del Monte and the next day playing to farm workers in Gilroy. It was while performing to such diverse audiences that Frawley honed his comic timing. Frawley could read an audience in seconds, and he would spice up the act with ad libs tailor-made just for the crowd he was playing for. The crowds ate it up.

In 1914, Frawley was smitten with San Diego native Edna Louise Broedt. Edna was six years younger than Frawley when they teamed up for the vaudeville stage. After a whirlwind, on-the-road courtship, the two married.

The couple performed a song and dance act, sprinkled with jokes, with Broedt playing the straight woman to Frawley's antics. Signed to the first-class Orpheum circuit, the pair performed at the best theaters in all the major cities.

In 1916, Bill picked up some extra money by acting in his first film, *Lord Loveland Discovers America*. In it, Frawley portrayed his first of many roles as a newspaper reporter. Later that year, Edna joined Bill in the silent film, *Persistent Percival*. She went on to film two more films that year without her husband, *Billy Van Deusen's Wedding Eve* and *A Gay Blade's Last Scrape*.

By the autumn of 1921, the Frawleys were separated. Their life had been one of nonstop traveling, rehearsing, and performing, which could not have been easy on the couple. It probably did not help matters that Bill was a loud, foulmouthed, two-fisted boozer, who at age thirty-four already looked like his future character, Fred Mertz. Edna quit show business and went back to San Diego. The couple divorced in December 1926. Neither Edna nor Bill ever remarried.

Being divorced suited Frawley fine. As far as he was concerned, men were men and women were for sex. He liked to socialize with men so that he could tell salty stories, play cards, talk sports, and drink without having a female pipe in. Bill loved all sports and had an encyclopedic knowledge of baseball. The only thing he loved more than drinking with other old-time performers was drinking with professional athletes and talking about sports.

Frawley next hit Broadway, where his little brother was enjoying a successful run on the boards. When Bill was not on stage or in rehearsal, he could be found in one of Manhattan's many swank speakeasies, drinking with members of the Yankees, Dodgers, and Giants. It was on Broadway that Frawley started to get a reputation for his penchant for intolerance and violence after he punched his co-star, Clifton Webb, in the nose during rehearsals for the 1928 production of *That's My Baby*. Webb, who was one of Broadway's most respected stars of that era and a closeted homosexual, angered Frawley with his prissy ways. Frawley was fired from the play.

Bill rebounded and continued to act on Broadway. From 1925 to 1933, he performed in nine Broadway plays, before moving to Hollywood. He was possibly motivated to make the move to a different medium by seeing his brother Paul's career fading on the Great White Way. Frawley was a working performer, and he was constantly on the watch for better opportunities and more money.

The film studios took to Frawley immediately, and, after making a film for Universal, the forty-six-year-old actor signed a seven-year contract with Paramount. He appeared in more than one hundred films between

1933 and 1951, usually playing cops, newspapermen, bartenders, coaches, and curmudgeons. His big films were the Bob Hope classic *The Lemon Drop Kid*; *Gentleman Jim*, with his drinking pal Errol Flynn; and the Charlie Chaplin film *Monsieur Verdoux*. His biggest role was in the Christmas classic, *Miracle on 34th Street*, where he appeared as the judge that freed Kris Kringle.

Hollywood fit Frawley well. He had a suite at the Knickerbocker Hotel, just off Hollywood Boulevard and close to his favorite watering holes. It suited him so well that he lived in the hotel for thirty years. He held court at the Brown Derby, the Musso and Frank Grill, and the Nickodell with the likes of Spencer Tracy, Pat O'Brien, and Bing Crosby, as well as professional boxers, baseball players, and even golfers.

To Frawley, Mexicans were Spics, African-Americans were Spades, and everyone else were Wops, Polacks, Krauts, or Limeys. His contempt for humanity had no prejudice; the slurs were just Frawley's way of seeing if you were one of the boys. If you had a hard time being addressed by an ethnic slur, Frawley made sure that you would not feel welcomed in the group. Fights would often break out when Bill was around, with the easily insulted Frawley often being restrained by the likes of Errol Flynn or Joe DiMaggio.

By the 1950s, Frawley's acting roles were drying up. Producers, directors, and fellow actors were wary of working with him. Although he was a professional first and foremost, his drinking and rude comments disturbed many in the film industry. Watching his bank account plunge, Frawley looked to the new media of television. Hearing that Hollywood knockabout Lucille Ball and her bandleader husband Desi Arnaz were looking to cast an old curmudgeon for the television program that they were producing, Frawley wasted no time contacting the pair.

Arnaz and Ball thought that Frawley would be perfect as their landlord and neighbor, Fred Mertz. Once the bigwigs at CBS found out about Frawley, they contacted Arnaz about their concerns over his behavior. Arnaz met with Frawley and told him of the network's issues.

"Well, those bastards," answered Frawley about the charges. "Those sonsabitches. They're always saying that about me. How the hell do they know, those bastards."

Arnaz wanted the cigar-chewing wise guy for the part, so he set some guidelines for Frawley: Three unexcused absences and he would be terminated. Frawley accepted the proposal, along with three hundred and fifty dollars a week. Also written into his contract was an October clause that allowed him to attend baseball's World Series every year. Frawley never missed a day on the set for the entire run of *I Love Lucy*.

Frawley's intolerance of the opposite sex was tested immediately, when stage actress Vivian Vance was selected for the role of Fred's wife, Ethel. Vance, who was a serious stage actress, was not exactly happy that she was paired up with Frawley. She felt that her character would never be married to a man Frawley's age. Vance, who had a reputation as a clotheshorse, was also unhappy with Ball's requirement that she be dressed in frumpy outfits, as well as having to weigh more than Lucy.

Vance and Frawley got did not get along. Vance thought Frawley was crude and disgusting. Frawley thought Vance was a stuck-up phony. In the early days, neither thought much about the future of the show, nor did they have any idea that *I Love Lucy* was going to be a huge hit and force them to work together for years. But being the true professionals that they were, they took the friction that they shared in real life and made it work for their characters, as they traded on-screen marital barbs at each other.

Frawley stayed to himself while on the program. He preferred to hide in his dressing room and away from the socializing on the set, where his humor and comments could easily be misconstrued. On most nights, Frawley could be found drinking at the Musso and Frank Grill, the revered Hollywood restaurant that was located right around the corner from the Knickerbocker Hotel.

Although he was earning more money than he had ever made in his life, Frawley stayed in his suite at the Knickerbocker Hotel. His little sister Mary moved in with him shortly after *I Love Lucy* became a hit. She kept him company, and she religiously attended the live tapings of the show. Mary died in 1957, at age fifty-nine.

Brothers Paul and John were in no shape to enjoy their brother's success. Both of them were hopeless alcoholics and were in the care of the St. John of God Hospital in Los Angeles. Frawley paid for their hospitalization for the rest of their lives.

One of the most frequently told stories about Frawley was about the time he took an unkempt panhandler to the Brown Derby Restaurant. Frawley was a regular there and was waved into the seating area, along with the bum. When Frawley ordered two scotch and sodas, the panhandler ordered the same, not knowing that Frawley was ordering for both of them. Frawley swore at him and punched him in the jaw, knocking him out cold.

During a rehearsal for *I Love Lucy*, Vance questioned Frawley's dancing abilities, which were required in the upcoming broadcast. Frawley delicately responded, "Well, for Chrissakes! I was in vaudeville since I was five years old and I guarantee you I'll wind up teaching old fat-ass how to do the fucking thing."

Their animosity toward each other became so heated that neither would accept script changes if one or the other wanted it. The irritated Frawley would often ask Arnaz, whom he called "Cuban," "Where the hell did you find this bitch?"

Television viewers had no idea that the actors despised one another. Frawley was nominated five times for an Emmy Award, but never won. Vance became the first actress to win an Emmy Award for Outstanding Supporting Actress and was nominated three more times while *I Love Lucy* was in production.

After the production of *I Love Lucy* concluded on May 6, 1957, Arnaz offered a television series reprising Frawley's and Vance's roles as Fred and Ethel Mertz. The new series meant big money for the actors, and the penny-pinching Frawley was eager to sign on to the project, even if that meant working with his nemesis. Vance quickly dismissed the idea, even turning down a fifty-thousand dollar signing bonus. She would not even film the pilot episode. Frawley was furious, which made Vance ecstatic.

At age seventy-three, Frawley was financially secure, as his contract with Arnaz paid him royalties in perpetuity. Most of the early television performers were paid royalties for only a couple of syndication runs, but Frawley's deal gave him royalties each and every time *I Love Lucy* was aired. Instead of spending his days watching his beloved Los Angeles Dodgers or hanging out with his pals at the Santa Anita Racetrack, Frawley did not know how not to work. His hobbies were expensive and he was always concerned about money.

Frawley landed another television acting role, this time on *My Three Sons* as Bub O'Casey, the maternal grandfather of the three young sons of widower Steven Douglas, played by movie star Fred McMurray. The show was a massive hit for the fledgling American Broadcast Corporation. Frawley's role was to be the housekeeper and comic foil for the boys and their misadventures. Unlike on *I Love Lucy*, Frawley took to the cast and was an endearing person to the young actors. Like a favorite uncle, Frawley told raunchy jokes, joined in on pranks, and taught the young cast how to drink. In a heartfelt gesture, Frawley bought cast member Stanley Livingston a top-quality surfboard for his birthday. The thought of Frawley shopping for surfboards cracked the cast up for weeks.

As apron-wearing Bub, Frawley was always cooking or cleaning, despite the fact that he had never cooked for anyone, even himself, for his entire adult life and had no idea how to act as if he were actually cleaning and cooking. Frawley did not care, as he was basically hired to play a censored version of himself and there was not an alcohol clause in his contract. Taking advantage of the loophole, Frawley usually drank his lunch at the nearby Nickodell Restaurant. The cast members were amazed at not just how much Frawley drank, but at the variety of drinks that he would consume. But he still hit his marks and cues after lunch.

To liven up *My Three Sons*, Steven Douglas needed to have an occasional girlfriend. One of them, Patricia Berry, caught Frawley's attention. Berry was a busy television actress, forty years younger than Frawley, but that did not stop a torrid affair from happening on and off the set during Berry's guest roles. Eventually, the married, brown-eyed, redheaded actress cooled off the relationship with Frawley, but not before word got out about the tryst.

When actress Joan Vohs was a guest on the show, Frawley caught a glimpse of the beautiful redhead walking past his dressing room. Frawley called director John Stephen over and asked him who the redhead was, and before Stephen could answer, Frawley added, "Oh boy, would I like to fuck her!" Stephen then informed Frawley that the redhead was his wife.

In one episode, a Native American was a guest on the show. The man never smiled the entire week of production, and that bothered Frawley to no end. All week long, Frawley tried to crack up the actor, but to no avail. Finally, while the last scenes were being filmed, the Native-American actor was filming a close-up when Frawley pulled out his penis and urinated on the floor within the actor's sightline. The actor completely lost his composure and laughed hysterically, along with the cast and crew.

*My Three Sons* sponsor Quaker Oats invited Frawley to the company's national convention as guest of honor and keynote speaker. The event was held in Frawley's dreaded Midwest, a place he had avoided for decades.

*My Three Sons* production manager John Stephens came with Frawley at Frawley's insistence. Frawley started drinking heavily the day of his speech. As the dinner dragged on, Frawley was almost blind drunk. A Quaker Oats executive got up to introduce Frawley and went on for too long, piling exaggerated compliments upon their esteemed guest of honor. Finally reaching the end of his introduction, the speaker introduced Frawley as "the greatest living American" to thunderous applause and a standing ovation. Frawley stumbled to the microphone and announced to the assembled mass, which included the executives' wives, the following:

"All right, I gotta tell ya this. I've been introduced in a lot of places, by a lot of people, but never, ever, have I heard so much shit piled so high as this last guy who introduced me. I don't know who the fuck you are, but you are really full of shit. Thank you and good night."

As *My Three Sons* progressed into its third year, Frawley began to show signs of failing health. He forgot lines and would fall asleep during filming. It got to the point where cast members were put next to Frawley so they could poke him in the back to wake him for his line.

Frawley did not pass his insurance physical for the 1964–65 season of *My Three Sons*. The doctor told producers that Frawley had suffered several strokes and should have been dead years ago. He was kept on for half the season until he was replaced with another hard-drinking, two-fisted actor, William Demarest. Bub was written out of the show with the explanation that he had moved to Ireland. Demarest was supposed to be Bub's brother, Charlie. The producers had wanted the two men to meet in Frawley's last episode, but it turned out that Demarest and Frawley had long hated one another and refused to work together.

Frawley occasionally visited the set after his release from the show, but his constant and vocal criticism of Demarest's work caused too much conflict, and Frawley was asked not to come back. With his health in rapid decline, Frawley moved out of the Knickerbocker, after having resided there for nearly thirty years, and into an apartment at 450 North Rossmore. He hired male nurses to help him around the clock with his medical and physical needs.

On the evening of March 3, 1966, William Frawley suffered a heart attack at the corner of Hollywood and Vine. His nurse carried him into the lobby of a nearby hotel and called an ambulance. Frawley was pronounced dead on arrival when he got to the Hollywood Receiving Hospital.

Desi Arnaz took out a full-page ad in the *Hollywood Reporter* for his friend. Along with his vital statistics and a photo of Frawley from his I Love Lucy days, the ad read only, "*Buenas Noches, Amigo!*"

Frawley's career spanned an amazing period in American entertainment history. He started out in pre-World War I vaudeville, was on Broadway in the twenties, in film in the thirties and forties, and on television in the fifties and sixties. He lived his life on his own terms, and he became famous at an age when most people retire from their careers.

Oddly, Frawley left the majority of his estate to actress Patricia Barry, his fling from *My Three Sons*.

# Chapter 28

## The Rebel

### Nick Adams—Los Angeles

Nick Adams was born Nicholas Aloysius Adamshock to Ukrainian immigrants in the hardscrabble coal mining town of Nanticoke, Pennsylvania, on July 10, 1931. After his uncle was killed in a mining accident, the family picked up and moved until they ran out of gasoline, ultimately ending up in Jersey City, New Jersey, where Adams spent the remainder of his childhood. Jersey City was not a paradise, and Adams was able to get off the streets by going to the movie theater as often as he could. He read movie fan magazines and dreamed of a better life than his parents had had. New York City was just across the river.

A chance meeting with an actor led Adams to an audition at Carnegie Hall, where he met the actor Jack Palance. After discovering that they were born in the same region of Pennsylvania, they struck up a friendship. Palance was Marlon Brando's understudy for *A Streetcar Named Desire* at the time and was doing fairly well for himself. He invited Adams up to his apartment and had sex with him. It was the first time that Adams had sex with a man, but it wouldn't be his last.

After a couple of weeks, Adams left Palance and hitchhiked to Hollywood. He landed a commercial for Coca-Cola and met the soon-to-be legendary James Dean. Dean and Adams became roommates and, allegedly, lovers. To make ends meet, they both hustled tricks on Santa Monica Boulevard. After tiring of the struggles of show business, Adams enlisted in the U.S. Coast Guard.

While on leave in San Diego, and dressed in his Coast Guard whites, Adams showed up for an audition for the Henry Fonda film *Mister*

*Roberts*. He got the part. After his military service was through, he returned to Hollywood and looked up his friend, James Dean.

Dean, whose star was rising, got Adams a small role in *Rebel Without a Cause*, and by all accounts Adams had sex with all three of its stars: Dean, Sal Mineo, and Natalie Wood. Wood's stage mother reportedly asked Adams to be Natalie's first sex partner, and he obliged.

Adams was devastated when James Dean died in a tragic auto crash on September 30, 1955. He began driving recklessly, racking up nine traffic violations in one year. It probably didn't help that enfant terrible Dennis Hopper was his housemate at the time.

Adams was getting more acting work in television and films just as Elvis Presley arrived in Hollywood, in 1956. Presley soon put out word that he wanted to meet James Dean's buddy. Adams and Presley quickly became friends, and Nick was Elvis' go-to man for anyone or anything he needed while in Los Angeles.

Presley and Adams were seen together all over Los Angeles, and many in the industry believed that Adams had latched onto Presley, as he had Dean, although Presley and Adams were allegedly more than just friends. When Elvis went back to Graceland, he left Nick an airline ticket to Memphis. The gossip columnists had a field day with their relationship. There was nothing the old-school show business people wanted more than to ruin the hillbilly outsider who was turning their children into rock 'n' roll maniacs. Knowing Adams' reputation as someone who would have sex with anyone who could advance his career, the gossip columnists spread rumors that Elvis and Nick were lovers.

To derail the rumors, Elvis' manager, Colonel Tom Parker, put Adams on the Elvis payroll while he toured. Parker, who was an illegal alien from the Netherlands, didn't like Adams and his big mouth. Adams had already told Elvis that the Colonel, who was taking a 50 percent cut of Elvis' fortune, was ripping him off, and the Colonel thought it would be better to have him on the payroll like the rest of Elvis' Memphis Mafia, or paid friends. Besides, as long as Elvis was having sex with Adams, the Colonel didn't need to worry about Elvis impregnating young women and paying for abortions. So close were the two that Adams was the only person allowed to visit Elvis in the days following the death of Elvis' mother, Gladys Presley.

### The Ballad of Johnny Yuma

A young Johnny Cash sang the "The Ballad of Johnny Yuma," the theme song of *The Rebel*. The song was released as a single a year after the program went off the air.

Adams landed a great part in the film *The Pajama Game*, starring Doris Day, Tony Randall, and Rock Hudson. The film was a romantic comedy, even though all of the leading men were gay. More film roles and television work fell into Adams' lap, and he no longer had to deal with the casting couches of film producers. During this time, Adams married former child actress Carol Nugent. Their marriage was filled with infidelities, mostly on Nugent's side of the bed. They had two children, Allyson Lee and Jeb Stuart.

Adams got his big break in 1959 with his role as Johnny Yuma in the television program *The Rebel*, which he also helped write. The show instantly became a hit with teenagers, who were attracted to the themes of rebellion, rejection, and justice. The show was also known as one of the most violent programs on television, and it was cancelled after its second season to placate the conservatives in Hollywood and Washington, D.C.

It wasn't long before Adams got a choice film role as a malicious murder suspect in the courtroom drama *Twilight of Honor*. Adams was nominated for best supporting actor at the 1963 Academy Awards, but lost to Melvyn Douglas for his role in *Hud*.

Adams' turbulent marriage came to an end in November 1966, when Nugent filed for divorce. The proceedings turned out to be expensive, as the couple fought over custody of their two children. Adams wasn't getting any younger, and his prematurely thinning hair made his teen rebel roles dry up. There were plenty of younger, cheaper actors in Hollywood to fill the void. Adams was reduced to acting in Japanese monster movies just to pay his attorney's fees.

With both his prospects and his bank account drying up, Adams paid a call on his old friend, Elvis. The two had had a falling-out in the early sixties over Adams' demand for money from Elvis. It was time to hit up Elvis again, this time with the threat of exposing his sexual secrets. The King threw Adams out of Graceland.

Word got out in Hollywood that Adams was threatening to write a tell-all book on the sexual preferences of very famous and powerful industry people. Adams was an avid journal keeper and had stacks of notebooks that contained all of the details of who, what, when, where, and how. The list of Adams' alleged sex partners is astonishing: besides Elvis, Jack Palance, James Dean, and Sal Mineo, there were also Joan Crawford, James Cagney, Rock Hudson, Rory Calhoun, Guy Madison, and director John Ford.

Nobody wanted to see the book written. Not only would it soil the careers of megastars, but millions of dollars would be lost on the bad publicity it would cause. John Wayne stopped by Adams' home at 2126 El Roble Drive in Beverly Hills to try to talk him out of writing the book and to warn him that it might get him killed. Wayne liked Adams and didn't want to see anything bad happen to him.

On February 7, 1968, Adams missed an appointment with his attorney, Ervin Roeder. The two were meeting to discuss negotiations with Colonel Tom Parker, who wanted to buy all of Adams' notebooks and his manuscript for his own personal library. Parker had spent a fortune over the years bribing editors, reporters, and young women and men not to report on Elvis' private life. Adams was just another brushfire to put out.

Roeder was concerned that Adams had missed the appointment, as he was always punctual. He drove to the actor's home and got no answer when he rang the doorbell. The house was all locked up, but Roeder managed to force open a window and crawl inside. He found Adams sitting in a chair in his upstairs bedroom. He was fully dressed and absolutely dead, his blue eyes staring across the room.

Dr. Thomas Noguchi, who later wrote two books about his career as the coroner of Los Angeles County from 1967 to 1982, performed the autopsy, and he certified the cause of death as "accidental-suicidal and undetermined." Massive doses of the sedative paraldehyde and the tranquilizer Promazine were found in Adams' body. He had a prescription for paraldehyde, but there was no evidence of any other drug in the rented home. Nor were any of Adams' notebooks, his manuscripts, his guns, or his typewriter found on the premises.

The police left it at that. Two of Adams' best friends, actors Broderick Crawford and Forrest Tucker, went to their graves believing that Adams had been murdered. However, Hollywood had nothing to gain from solving the mysterious death of a rebel.

# Only in California

*Today, over thirty-seven million people live in California, more than in any other state. California is also four times bigger in area than Ohio, so it's just a matter of numbers that nutty things happen here. Non-Californians like to point out that we are a bunch of wine-sipping, granola-eating liberals; however, we have more beer-swilling, BBQ-eating rednecks than most states have people. Between the two, we have more fruits, flakes, and nuts than anywhere else in America.*

# Chapter 29

## The Terror Bandit

### Clarence "Buck" Kelly—San Francisco

The evening of October 9, 1926, was a beautiful night in San Francisco, where the low clouds and scattered rain showers scrubbed the industrial grime off the urban landscape. The Saint Louis Cardinals had tied up the World Series by trouncing the New York Yankees ten to two in game six. Los Angeles-based evangelical Christian preacher Aimee Semple McPherson was in court for obstructing justice over her faked kidnapping earlier that year. Herman "Rudolph" Suhr, who served twelve years in prison for the murder of Yuba County district attorney E. T. Maxwell during the Wheatland Hop Riot of 1913, was granted parole on the condition that he find what the parole board regarded as suitable work.

Sometime around nine in the evening, Clarence "Buck" Kelly and Lawrence Weeks, both twenty-two years old, along with two unidentified young men, drank some homemade alcohol and stole an automobile. After driving to a hardware store on Vallejo Street, they asked owner Joseph Calonico to show them some handguns. When the unsuspecting Calonico handed them a .38 caliber revolver that they asked to see, Calonico was struck multiple times by the pair, who then took the gun, along with ammunition. The two unidentified men made what was probably one of the best decisions in their young lives—they ran off, leaving Weeks and Kelly to commit their crimes without their help.

With robbery on their drunken minds, the pair drove to Guillen's Pool Hall at 1968 Lombard Street. Inside, Kelly asked owner Constantio Guillen for a package of cigarettes. When Guillen turned his back to retrieve the cigarettes, Kelly hit him on the head with his revolver and fired five bullets into his prone body. Weeks violently rounded up the seven patrons, who just moments earlier had been enjoying a Saturday night, and lined them up against a wall. They robbed the men of their money and valuables before fleeing into the foggy night. Guillen died the next day.

The crime spree began in earnest, as the pair stopped Mario Pagano on Powell Street and attempted to rob him. Pagano resisted and was shot dead for his trouble. The police found thirty dollars in his wallet.

Looking for an easier target, Kelly and Weeks spotted George Karaisky, Beth Bolu, Emma Bird, and her fourteen-year old daughter, Emma, strolling on Bryant Street near 8th Street. After relieving the group of their money and valuables, Weeks and Kelly forced the elder Bird into their car and drove off. They threw her out of the car at 10th and Bryant, telling her that they did not like her looks.

Mario Begene was savagely gunned down when he did not have enough money to suit the pair. He died two days later. The pair cruised through San Francisco, looking for more victims to rob. They relieved Harry Gianini of twenty-eight dollars at the intersection of Steiner and Sutter. Next, they robbed Lester Irish at Webster and Washington streets, taking a miserly four dollars and thirty-five cents.

Seeking more crimes of opportunity, the men spotted John Copren fumbling with his keys at 1914 Pine Street and robbed him of ten dollars in front of his home. Using the same technique, the pair robbed Dr. S. Nicholas Jacobs of a four hundred and fifty-dollar watch and ninety-five dollars in front of his home on Webster Street. Shortly after that crime, Anthony Ganzales was robbed of his coat and twenty dollars at 5th and Harrison. One block down Harrison Street, Weeks and Kelly robbed Manual Salazar of sixteen dollars.

Before calling it a night, Kelly and Weeks relieved Jack Story and Henry Berthiaune of cash and their watches in front of their home at 1225 Clay Street.

After lying low for a day—probably sleeping off his hangover—Buck Kelly met up with a friend of a friend, seventeen-year-old Mike Papadaches. After drinking some bootleg alcohol together, they decided to repeat another night of terrorizing San Francisco. Around six in the evening, they called a Yellow Cab, with evil intentions on their minds.

Kelly had worked the previous summer as a cab driver, so it is possible that he recognized the cabbie who picked them up. Roy Swanson, an insurance salesman, husband, and father of a one-month-old-baby girl, was driving a Yellow Cab to make extra money. Swanson, who was probably jovial to have an acquaintance as a fare, was soon shocked when Kelly ordered him to stop on the 16th Street viaduct. Kelly ordered Swanson out of his cab at gunpoint. While Papadaches rifled through Swanson's cashbox, Kelly ask Swanson for his Yellow Cab jacket and cap. Swanson gave Kelly his uniform and was promptly shot. Swanson and Papadaches tossed Swanson's dead body off the viaduct and drove into the Mission District.

Kelly and Papadaches pulled the cab up alongside Nicholas Petrovitch at San Bruno and Mariposa Streets and asked him for the time of day. Petrovitch, who was enjoying an after-dinner walk, pulled out his watch and told them the time. Kelly shot and killed him.

After driving a few blocks, the killers stopped at a restaurant at 7th and Brannan Streets. Cook Louis Fernandez was standing at the entrance of the restaurant, taking a break from his duties when Kelly and Papadaches walked up to him. Kelly stuck his revolver in Fernandez's face and told him to "hold up his hands." Fernandez, not believing the audacity of the bandits, replied, "You're joking."

"Joking?" replied Kelly. "Damn you! Take that!"

Fernandez heard the trigger click, followed by a loud report, and he felt a sharp pain in his neck.

After taking forty dollars from the cash register, Kelly and Papadaches dashed across Brannan Street to a gas station and ordered C. W. Johnson to put up his hands. Johnson did what he was told, but the jumpy Kelly shot him in the neck after Johnson made a gesture of resistance.

Johnson's friends, Rex Hayder and Jack Duane, jumped the killers and tried to overpower them, but they were both shot multiple times, with Duane dying immediately on the oily asphalt. Johnson crawled out into the intersection, where two marine engineers took him to the hospital, not knowing about the other victims.

Kelly and Papadaches drove to Pier 86, where they viciously attacked marine pilot Alvin Anderson. He was pistol-whipped, robbed of his money, and left in a bloody heap on the sidewalk.

The violent duo then drove to another gas station, this one at 3rd and Mariposa, where they robbed the register and beat attendant Steve Walker. The owner of the station, L. O. Strand, called the police.

Officer Dorsey Henderson was nearby and answered the call. Seeing the parked cab with the offenders inside, and well aware of the ongoing crime spree, Henderson opened fired on the vehicle, which had begun to move away from the curb. The cab crashed into a curb, and Kelly and Papadaches bailed out, firing at Officer Henderson while they ran to the nearby railroad yard. Minutes later, the suspects reappeared, driving past Henderson in a second car that they had apparently stolen at the railroad yard. Both parties exchanged shots at one another.

This was to be the last time that the Terror Bandits would be on the loose in San Francisco. The police wasted no time in trying to apprehend Kelly and Papadaches. Police dragnets were thrown up all over the San Francisco Bay Area. Small towns formed posses to man roadblocks and protect their towns from the Terror Bandits. Every usual suspect from Monterey to Santa Rosa was hauled to police stations for questioning. Finally, on October 17, Patrick Wafer, a hard-boiled detective sergeant, cornered one of his underworld connections and got the hoodlum to give him a lead. Since we're talking about the pre-Miranda Rights days, you can use your imagination to figure out how Sergeant Detective Wafer got his information.

Lawrence Weeks was picked up at five in the afternoon on October 18 by detectives as he left his construction job at the Duboce Tunnel. After being interrogated by San Francisco's finest, Weeks gave the police Kelly's name and address.

Detective sergeants George Wall, William McMahon, and Leo Bunner led a squad of patrolmen to Kelly's squalid apartment at 47 South Park Street. As the police fumbled their way through the dimly lit hallway, Kelly bolted out of his flat and ran to the back stairway and down the exterior stairway.

The police, not about to take chances on a man who had already murdered six people, opened fired on the fleeing Kelly as he ran down the wooden stairs. Wounded and bleeding, Kelly ran into the ground floor apartment of a Mexican family and hid in their closet, where he was easily taken into custody soon afterward. In Kelly's room, police detectives found a bloody shirt and Swanson's leather puttees, part of his Yellow Cab uniform.

Kelly, who was shot in the thumb and lungs, was taken to Central Emergency Hospital where he was deemed in critical condition. Surgery was necessary, but Kelly refused the operation, saying, "I'm picked as the fall guy. Why should I get patched up here so that the police can swing me off later? I'd rather die right here!"

Kelly's mother, Katherine Kelly, and her daughter, eighteen-year-old Edna, were brought to the hospital by the police to talk him into the operation. Kelly kept up his bravado. He told his mother, "I'm the fall guy, Ma. All my life I've been the fall guy. Why should I let them operate? They'll patch me up and then they'll hang me. What's the use? I'd rather die here."

Katherine Kelly reminded her son that he had a wife and child to think about. He changed his mind about dying for the sake of his two-month-old daughter, Dorothy, and his wife, Alma.

Even though Papadaches was still unidentified and on the loose, the newspapers had a field day reporting the capture of the Terror Bandits. They called Kelly a human tiger and printed whatever spewed out of his mouth. Kelly, maintaining his complete innocence, called Weeks a "rat" and a "hophead"—old-time slang for a marijuana user.

Clarence "Buck" Kelly was charged with four counts of first degree murder and was tried separately from Papadaches and Weeks. Assistant District Attorney Isadore Golden believed it to be easiest to convict him with the May 11 murders of Jack Duane, Walter Swanson, and Michael Petrovich. Kelly entered a plea of not guilty by reason of insanity.

Kelly's attorney was Milton U'Ren, the tough former assistant district attorney who, in 1922, was assigned to prosecute film star Roscoe "Fatty" Arbuckle for the murder of film extra and prostitute Virginia Rappe. Even with such a competent attorney as U'Ren, Kelly was doomed to the hangman's rope because of the testimony of his accomplices and victims.

Papadaches was unbreakable on the witness stand. The seventeen-year old stanchly told the court of the events of October 11. The two met at Kelly's apartment at 47 South Park Street around midday, when they started on an all-day drinking binge. Taking taxis on their tour of various San Francisco speakeasies and pool halls, the two had a thoroughly drunken time. A third person, who Papadaches only knew as "Span," joined them for a time, eating at a restaurant at Twenty-Eighth and Mission with the pair and sharing a cab to a pool hall on Third Street, where they continued drinking before calling the Yellow Cab that Swanson was driving.

*The San Francisco Examiner* wrote that Kelly acted completely aloof, while Papadaches told what he could remember of the evening. The paper reported that Papadaches' "beady black eyes," rolled while Papadaches testified.

Whether he was merely acting to appear mentally defective during the incriminating testimony, Kelly could not hold back his rage when Weeks took the stand to testify a few days later. It was reported in *The San Francisco Chronicle* that Kelly's face turned red, and his nose and jaw twitched uncontrollably, while Weeks told his version of their activities on the night of May 9.

If it were not bad enough that Kelly's partners in crime testified against him, Kelly was shocked to find out that a passerby, Peter McPhee, had witnessed Kelly shooting Swanson on the 16th Street viaduct. McPhee was about a block away and had a clear view of the crime. Seeing Swanson gunned down terrified McPhee, who ran from the scene as fast as he could.

Kelly had more surprises in store for him when two of his friends, Roy O'Neal and James Fitzgerald, both told the court that shortly before the May 9 reign of terror, Kelly had told them, "I'm going over the gate soon, but I'm sure going to raise hell in San Francisco before I go." To make matters worse for Kelly, Fitzgerald and O'Neal recalled that they saw Kelly on Sunday, October 10, at a speakeasy at Third and Hanson where he bragged to the pair that, "Well, they didn't think I'd get them, but I did. Didn't I?"

Louis Fernandez, the cook who Kelly shot at the restaurant, and Rex Hayder, who came to the aid of his friend, C. W. Johnson, when Kelly attempted to rob the gas station at Seventh and Brannan, also testified at the trial, indicting Kelly as the murderer. Both men had been shot point-blank by Kelly, and they were both still recovering from their bullet wounds. Their testimony doomed any hope of Kelly being found not guilty, except by reason of insanity.

Clarence "Buck" Kelly took the stand in his own defense. U'Ren questioned him about the nights of October 9 and 11, and Kelly answered that he could not remember anything about the nights in question. He claimed that after consuming a few drinks, he would lose his memory. Most of his replies were limited to a terse, "I guess."

U'Ren questioned Kelly about the many head injuries that he had incurred during his twenty-two years of life. Kelly testified that when he was a child he suffered a skull fracture due to a fall. As an adolescent he was knocked unconscious by a flying object, and he was also kicked in the mouth by a horse when he was a teenager. He had also been an amateur boxer, with fifteen matches under his belt. Kelly claimed—but oddly no doctor testified for the defense—that he had a three-inch, unhealed crack in his skull.

Assistant District Attorney Isadore Golden angered Kelly during the cross-examination. Kelly was defiant, and he shouted his answers back at Golden. At one point, it appeared that Kelly was going to leap out of the witness stand to attack the district attorney.

U'Ren had Kelly's mother, Margaret Kelly, and his aunt, Marjorie McClelland, testify on Clarence's behalf. Margaret told the jury that Clarence's father, also named Clarence, was an insane, alcoholic criminal, who was currently incarcerated at San Quentin Prison. The sisters also verified the many head injuries that Kelly had suffered.

During the prosecution's rebuttal, Doctor Joseph Catton was put on the stand and announced that Kelly's head injuries would not cause him to have amnesia. Dr. Catton stated that "there was no damage to his skull and no permanent affliction of the brain from his prior accidents."

The case went to the jury on December 21. The jurors came back after deliberating only twenty minutes, and they delivered a verdict of guilty.

"Well, they can't break my spirit," said Kelly, as he was led away in handcuffs by the bailiff.

Doctor Leo L. Stanley was the son of a San Miguel country doctor and was expected to replace his father after he finished his studies at Stanford's medical school. His father's premature death made it financially difficult for the young Stanley to finish college without having to take time off to work menial jobs in order to save for tuition. It took him eight years to graduate. Finding himself working as an unpaid intern at a San Francisco hospital, he applied for a job as the assistant physician at San Quentin Prison, twelve miles north of San Francisco in Marin County. He was hired in February 1913, and by August of that year, he became the resident physician. Stanley held that position for twenty-seven years.

Stanley was a progressive in his philosophy. He believed that there were only a few true criminals in San Quentin; the rest were uneducated, unskilled, and mentally or physically ill.

Even though the doctor was a progressive in his policies toward the prisoners, he was not easily fooled, and he often had to deal violently with prisoners with escape on their minds. Stanley was fair, but he was physically tougher than most of the prisoners and the guards.

Doctor Stanley first met Clarence "Buck" Kelly when the infamous criminal was transferred to San Quentin from San Francisco City Jail in February 1927. Because of his notoriety, most of the hospital staff attended Kelly's initial physical examination. Kelly reveled in the attention, swaggering and acting like a tough guy while standing completely naked in the clinic. Stanley noted that Kelly was in perfect physical condition despite having admitted to smoking marijuana. His good facial features were marred only by a misaligned nose and an evasive and shifty expression.

During the examination, Kelly asked Stanley if it "was true that they take the brains out of all the guys that they hang here?" The doctor explained that scientists had been able to collect valuable scientific information from the autopsies of the condemned men. According to Stanley, Kelly looked thoughtful, then gave a contemptuous laugh and replied: "Well, you can take mine out and cremate the rest of me, for all I care. I'm a con and my old man's a con, and nobody gives a damn about me. I should worry after it's all over!" Kelly's father was in San Quentin's ward for the mentally deficient. Forty-four years old, the senior Kelly appeared to be a much older man and was mentally confused, possibly from the advanced stages of syphilis and alcoholism.

Kelly's mother visited her son as often as she could. Stanley described her as a kind and simple woman, wearing worn-out clothing, who adored her eldest child.

Buck Kelly swaggered into the execution room on May 11, 1928. Doctor Stanley, the attending physician, wrote of the event:

> When Buck came into the execution room, he was still "the buck," swaggering and debonair. He seemed flattered by the large group of

> witnesses waiting before the gallows. One hundred and fifty had come to see him hang. Vanity cannot climb San Quentin's thirteen steps and survive. By the time Buck reached the rap, his courage was gone. There was a ghastly delay when the hangman's thumb caught in the noose. As they drew the black cap down over the "Terror Bandit's" face, I heard him call out like a frightened kid: "Good-by, mother."

The trapdoor of the gallows was sprung at 10:04 a.m. and Dr. Stanley declared him dead fourteen minutes later.

A small scandal arose after reports emerged that Kelly's brain had been removed during the autopsy for study, against Kelly wishes. Dr. Stanley had to defend both himself and San Quentin's practice of studying the brains of executed criminals. He was cleared of any wrongdoing after Margaret Kelly received monetary compensation.

# Chapter 30

## Black and White and Read All Over

### Harry French—Alturas, Modoc County

You'd be hard-pressed to find a more isolated town in California than Alturas in Modoc County. Located high in the upper right-hand corner of the Golden State on lonesome Highway 395, Alturas is the last bit of civilization for fifty miles to the Oregon border. The Nevada state line is situated fifteen miles to the east on Highway 299. At 4,370 feet above sea level, this arid place exists only because the Pitt River supplied that rarity in the Great Basin, water. If Alturas seems remote now, in 1937 it was like being on another planet.

Gertrude Payne was the editor of the *Alturas Plain Dealer*, the paper of record in Modoc County. Payne's husband, Robert "Bard" French, served as business manager, and together they had an iron grip on vital statistics and court-enforced public announcements, which are a windfall to small-town newspapers. Longtime residents of Modoc County, the Frenches enjoyed a good living at the top of the social ladder in Alturas.

Claude McCracken and his wife moved to Alturas in the mid-1930s. Along with his business partner, twenty-seven-year-old Donna Conwell, McCracken started up a mimeographed, eight-page biweekly called the *Modoc Mail*. McCracken was also the local representative of the United Press and the Associated Press.

McCracken's paper openly taunted the *Plain Dealer* for not publishing local news. McCracken thought the *Plain Dealer* was a powder-puff newspaper, heavy on the social activities of the elite of Modoc County. A feud erupted between Payne and McCracken that spilled over into their newspapers, something McCracken thoroughly enjoyed.

McCracken wrote editorials criticizing the French family's nepotism in Modoc County politics. Payne's brother, Jim, worked for the national reemployment service. Her daughter worked for the state, as well as her son, twenty-seven-year-old Harry French, who was employed by the State Board of Equalization. On April 5, 1935, McCracken published a piece in the *Modoc Mail* titled "Panaceas and Painkillers" (the alliteration was a play on the family name Payne). The author of the article wrote that he always believed "that a person addicted to grandiose ideas … always suggested … that anything couldn't be done … without their aid … One of our modern painkillers … in Alturas … you know who I mean … has always insisted … that it was in business … because of some God- given right … which accidentally precipitated … the perpetrators of this rag … into this region … a hundred years ago."

McCracken was playing hardball against the *Plain Dealer*. He railed against the cozy relationship that Gertrude Payne had with county officials, never reporting on alleged wrongdoings and sweetheart deals. He poked fun at her family and social connections. On January 23, 1936, the *Modoc Mail* published a piece which contained the following:

> My dear Gertrude: Here is a letter to the editor which you will not print because it isn't a bouquet.
>
> In your last issue you made the assertion that one "overzealous" reporter sent the report to the press that Alturas was under water, etc., etc. Now, Gertrude, you shouldn't have done that, because when you did you uttered and published a malicious lie, wholly without foundation, in fact, something you might have verified by asking a few questions before rushing into print. I have no scruples in calling a woman (notice I didn't say a lady) a liar, so I hereby notify you that you are an unscrupulous, infamous, notorious and utterly indefensible liar. I might sue you for libel, but a judgment against you would be worth about as much as six bits in confederate money. I really shouldn't waste my time calling you on this because you can't get as little a thing as the appointment of Dr. John Stile as Superintendent of the hospital correct when that appointment is published on the minutes of the Supervisors. I naturally assume that you are accustomed to popping off your mouth without regard to truth.

> You may consider this a written notice to you to keep my name, or any reference to me, out of that sheet you erroneously term a newspaper.
>
> I am also signing this with a salutation you can't imitate.
>
> Yours truly, Claude L. McCracken.

Gertrude was no angel, either. Besides her own comments criticizing McCracken, the *Plain Dealer* published an account of a husband and wife named McCracken who were arrested in Reno for narcotic possession—not exactly local news, as Reno is more than 140 miles south of Alturas. This was especially vile because McCracken's wife worked as a registered nurse at the Alturas hospital.

Gertrude's son Harry was a fragile man, both mentally and physically. He lived with his parents until he married at the age of twenty-five. Following his family tradition of preferential treatment, he landed a job with the California State Board of Equalization, but he did not have to move to Sacramento, or even to Chico. Amazingly, Harry was assigned to Modoc County.

Harry had grown up in the family newspaper business, and even though he was a married father with a good state job, he remained heavily involved with the day-to-day operations. In the September 8, 1936, issue of the *Modoc Mail*, McCracken taunted Harry with this quip: "Some folks are wondering if Sales Tax Harry is French, Latin or Greek. One more cent, please." McCracken later wrote in a column titled "Rambling Around" that a local representative of the State Board of Equalization had been fired for incompetency. Since Harry was the only representative of the Board of Equalization in Modoc County, he angrily stormed into the *Modoc Mail*'s office to confront McCracken about the article. McCracken flippantly replied that Harry's name did not appear in the column and there was nothing that he could do about it. Harry was livid.

McCracken was up to his old tricks in the March 25, 1937 issue of the *Modoc Mail* when he published in his column an innuendo that implied that one of the French's ancestors was lynched for stealing horses in Montana. Harry read the article while at The Tavern, a social club that, as the name says, was just a private tavern with Ping-Pong tables, billiards, and beer. Harry's friends told him that it was no big deal, but Harry stewed over the article while becoming increasingly inebriated. Stumbling drunk, Harry walked into a secondhand store and borrowed a pistol.

Around 6:30 p.m., McCracken, Conwell, and Evelyn Olen, a family friend, were sitting at the kitchen table eating dinner when Harry pulled up in front of the McCracken home. Two teenagers who lived across the street saw Harry get out of his car and fall down into the winter mud and slush. Stumbling to his feet, Harry walked into the home, went into the kitchen and shot McCracken five times. McCracken got up, walked to the sink, and collapsed.

Harry French walked to the house next door and told the resident, a man that he had known his entire life, that he had just shot McCracken. The man at first did not believe him, but he was soon convinced by the commotion coming from next door. Deputy Sheriff George Kelley was the first to arrive and promptly arrested French. On the way to the jail, Officer Kelley asked French why he had shot McCracken. French's answer was straightforward. "That son of a bitch insulted my folks," he replied. "There is some things people can't stand, George. I just stood more than I could stand."

Always the newsman, McCracken dictated the shooting to Conwell for the wire services while he was being loaded into an ambulance. At the hospital, McCracken's wife was on duty and fainted when she heard the news. She bravely helped the doctors try to save his life, but it was too late. McCracken died a few hours after the incident.

Once faced with the death penalty, Harry French changed his plea to insanity. With a jury composed of his friends and neighbors, French was found guilty in an amazingly quick trial. The ranchers on the jury wanted to get back to their spread, as there was work to be done.

On July 19, 1937 French was sentenced to life and sent to San Quentin Prison. French appealed his conviction in 1941 and lost. His sentence was later reduced to make him eligible for parole, which he eventually gained.

Harry French died in Sacramento on January 20, 1974, almost thirty-seven years after he assassinated Claude McCracken.

# Chapter 31

## Big Daddy

### Eric Nord—San Francisco/Venice

Eric "Big Daddy" Nord was a giant of a man, standing six foot, eight inches and weighing around three hundred pounds. Nord was born as Harry Helmuth Pastor in 1919 to an American mother and a German father in Krefeld, Germany. When he was fifteen years old, Pastor emigrated to the United States, settling in Los Angeles where he took acting classes and changed his name to Eric Nord. He arrived in San Francisco in the early 1940s, married, had four children, and divorced.

Big Daddy embraced the bohemian lifestyle that was appearing in postwar San Francisco. Disillusioned young people, many of them veterans of World War II, rejected the workaday world and the brash consumerism that overwhelmed the so-called "greatest generation." The Beats created art, music, poetry, and literature and worked menial jobs far below their education level to live in spartan studio apartments and drink cheap wine. As with any group of intellectual and creative movements, there were many marginally talented artists, hangers-on, and lost souls who would be misfits in any society. For every Allen Ginsberg, Richard Brautigan, and Jack Kerouac, there were dozens of Beats who drove cabs, sold fish, or were just not that talented. Eric Nord had a talent for self-promotion.

When Nord worked, he helped out at the Co-Existence Bagel Shop at 1398 Grant Street in the North Beach neighborhood. The bagel store/ coffee shop was an all-around happening place for beatniks in San Francisco.

In 1950, Nord rented a basement at 599 Jackson Street and opened an unlicensed nightclub that he named The Hungry i. The nightly drunken revelry cause too many police raids, so Nord sold the lease to Enrico Banducci, who turned The Hungry i into the launching pad for such comedians as Phyllis Diller, Jonathan Winters, Dick Gregory, Bill Cosby, Woody Allen, Lenny Bruce, Dick Cavett, and Mort Sahl.

While Beats like Bob Kauffman and Kenneth Rexroth were working hard on their craft, Nord was hosting wild parties at his Produce District building that was called the Party Pad. Strictly a "bring your own beverage" setting, it was constantly raided by the San Francisco Police Department as a public nuisance where drinking, dancing, and poetry readings raged to wild bebop jazz. The press reported that young white women mingled with black men, homosexuals cavorted with each other, and widespread drug use was the norm at the Party Pad. The police responded by infiltrating the loosely knit group and increasing patrols in North Beach. Police surveillance often turned into harassment as San Francisco's finest brought it onto themselves to stop interracial beatnik couples from mingling together on the street.

In 1958, the Pulitzer Prize–winning *San Francisco Chronicle* columnist Herb Caen named the North Beach nonconformists "beatniks," and crowned Nord the "King of Beatniks." The term was rejected by the bohemians, but Nord, knowing that all publicity was good publicity, ran with his moniker.

At approximately 3:45 a.m. on June 16, 1958, taxi driver/saxophonist Paul B. Swanson fell from the roof of the Party Pad and died. If that wasn't bad enough, two days later, Swanson's girlfriend, twenty-year old Connie Sublette, was found raped and murdered in an alley between 432 and 436 Lyon Street, near Golden Gate Park. Sublette was well-known among San Francisco's bohemians. At one time or another, she had been kicked out of every hangout in North Beach. She was known for getting wildly drunk and occasional public nudity.

After viewing Swanson's body in his coffin, Sublette got blazing drunk, eventually going to her estranged husband's apartment at 426 Lyon Street. Having no key, Swanson sat on the steps of the apartment, sobbing loudly, until the apartment manager told her to leave before he called the cops. Thirty-three-year-old seaman Frank Harris, who had just shot up heroin, witnessed the commotion and walked Swanson away from the building and into an alley where he raped and strangled the poor girl.

The press was outraged over the murder of the trust fund–financed beatnik, but good, old-fashioned police work caught the killer. Harris, an African American, had hurried to his ship, the *U.S.S. Gaffey*, after realizing that he had dropped the receipt for a new suit that he had just bought at the scene of the crime. He waited on board for the police to arrest him. The detectives cuffed him just two hours before his ship was to set sail to Asia.

Meanwhile, life went on as ever at the Party Pad. On June 21, 1958, San Francisco police raided the club again. They arrested seven people. Nord was arrested for operating a public dance hall without a license and for unpaid traffic citations going back to 1952.

Nord's devil-may-care attitude toward social norms again got him into trouble after he and twenty-four year old Thomas Lawrence went on the road for four days with two underage females. The two men were involved in the Leonard Bernstein one-act opera *Trouble in Tahiti* at Marines' Memorial Theater. Lawrence was the set director and Nord acted as the narrator.

The two somehow met sixteen-year-old ward of the state Dyanne Anderson and seventeen-year-old Penny Nicolai after the show and drove off with them in Nord's Oldsmobile. They allegedly went to the village of Mill Valley in Marin County, where Nord had friends, and later they went to Big Sur, where they took a steam bath. Nord and Lawrence were oblivious to the all-points bulletin put out on the missing girls until they picked up a newspaper on August 10.

Nord got back just in time to join the Squaresville Tour. Tired of the tourist tours through North Beach pointing out beatnik hangouts, someone hired a bus, hung out a Squaresville Tour banner on the side, and drove up to the Saint Francis Hotel. The bus load of beatniks walked into the lobby of the expensive hotel with drums, bongos, and flutes playing. They held signs that read, "The Beats are touring the bourgeois wasteland" and "Hi, squares, the citizens of North Beach are on tour."

With San Francisco's finest following close behind, the tour moved on to the elegant salon of I. Magnin, where they put on their own fashion show. Finally, they ended up at Union Square, where they read poetry aloud.

Sometime during the tour, police detectives arrested Nord for contributing to the delinquency of a minor. Nicolai and Anderson both told the authorities that no alcohol, sex, or drugs were involved in the outing. The only thing that happened was that the girls dyed their hair black. Nord was released on a one thousand–dollar bond.

The San Francisco Police Department turned up the heat on Big Daddy on August 19, 1958. He was arrested for bouncing two checks totaling two hundred and five dollars at a Los Angeles dress shop. Nord told the press, "I just bought a couple of dresses for a chick down there."

Nord finished up his legal trouble near the end of the year. Fined three hundred dollars and put on three years' probation, Nord was told by Judge Melvyn Cronin that "he would not tolerate any deviation from proper conduct." He ordered Nord to get a job, pay off his debts, and to try to conform a little more to society.

Nord filed for bankruptcy and, along with girlfriend Julie Meredith, moved to Venice, California, where they started a new beatnik coffee house at 1501 Ocean Front Walk. Located right on the beach on the site of the former Mecca Buffet, The Gas House was financed by civil liberties attorney Al Matthews, who also rented out the top floor of the nearby Grand Hotel for his staff. Successful journalist and beat poet Lawrence Lipton was the creative director. Poet John Thomas was the manager and cook. Nord was the greeter and emcee.

Venice, a beach district on the western fringe of Los Angeles, was a failed town at the time. Its canals, which were supposed to be the pinnacle feature of the subdivision, were stagnant and contaminated with sewage. Boarded up businesses sat next to seedy hotels and dodgy taverns. Oil wells studded the entire district, situated right up to the beach. It appeared to be the perfect spot for the nonconformist bohemians and beat types from all over southern California who moved to Venice.

The Gas House was the place to be. Lipton and Thomas led nightly poetry readings. Poets Frank Rios, Clair Horner, Shanna Moore, and Philomene Long read their poems at The Gas House. Jack Kerouac, Ken Kesey, and the folk group Peter, Paul, and Mary were known to hang out at The Gas House when they were in Los Angeles, as well as were young actors from nearby Hollywood.

When two thousand people showed up for an event at The Gas House, the Los Angeles media picked up the story and stirred up beatnik hysteria. The bearded, unkempt, and quotable beatniks were the kind of thing that the newspapers, radio, and television could not get enough of.

Beatniks made good copy, and the colorful and unabashed Nord was, after all, Big Daddy, the King of the Beatniks, fresh off his sentencing for his wild weekend with the teenage females up north.

The city did everything it could to close down The Gas House. Eventually, it succeeded by deeming the coffee shop an unlicensed dance club on April 1, 1960. Subsequently,The Gas House was made into an art gallery, but it continued to be harassed by the local government until it closed a few years later. Nord's cash cow was gone and he had to find real work.

Nord turned to private detective work, carpentry, real estate, and acting to pay his bills. He took small roles in the B-movies *Once Upon a Knight*, *The Flower Thief*, and *The Hypnotic Eye*. Despite all the talk coming out of Big Daddy's mouth, his film career was over before he started.

In 1965, Nord, along with Santa Cruz clinical psychologist Leon Tabory, opened the legendary underground concert venue, The Barn, in nearby Scott Valley. Part coffee shop, bookstore, and concert venue, bands like the Grateful Dead, Country Joe and the Fish, and Janis Joplin performed there. Ken Kesey's Merry Pranksters made The Barn a stop on their Electric Kool-Aid Acid Test tour. Legend has it that the supergroup Led Zeppelin performed at The Barn during its first American tour; however, the heavy metal band did not actually exist while The Barn was in operation.

Scott Valley was a sleepy farm town and the residents did not like the noise, the traffic, nor the unkempt beatniks who occupied their town on the weekends. Legal harassment began. Tabory was arrested and tried for selling obscene literature, but was acquitted. Finally, in 1968, The Barn lost its lease and was taken over by the Baymonte Christian School. The murals were painted over and the structure was turned into a student dormitory. In 1982, what had once been The Barn became part of an RV campsite.

Nord, whose weight was now topping four hundred pounds, began to slow down. He purportedly opened a cultural center in San Francisco's Haight-Ashbury neighborhood in the early 1970s. He eventually moved to Santa Clara County, residing in Los Gatos, where it was rumored that he owned bohemian coffee shops in various Bay Area enclaves. Toward the end of his life, he enjoyed playing Santa Claus in Los Gatos during Christmas time. He died there in 1989.

# Chapter 32

## The Educated Idiot

### John Russell Crooker—Bel Air

Many occupations barely exist anymore: blacksmith, barrel maker, typewriter repair. Houseboy is another occupation that you rarely hear of anymore. A houseboy was a personal domestic servant, usually a person of color, who was more of an assistant than butler. Even in the 1950s' high society, the houseboy was no longer fashionable. So, it is puzzling how thirty-four-year-old John Russell Crooker, a married, UCLA law student and father of two, became employed by a Bel Air heiress as her houseboy. But he did, and that's when things got really interesting.

Crooker had found his sugar mama in thirty-three-year-old divorcee, Norma McCauley. The daughter of millionaire contractor J. A. Thompson and mother of three, McCauley was born into Los Angeles' elite. As a wedding present, Thompson built for Norma and her husband, former Air Force major and air ace Frank McCauley, a dream house that was equipped with every modern convenience then known to man. They lived the life that most people only see in the movies. Spectacular mansions, expensive cars, and fancy parties were all Norma McCauley knew.

Things turned sexual between McCauley and Crooker and it was not long before Crooker wanted to be more than McCauley's houseboy. Crooker now had a taste of the good life and wanted in. Norma looked like his meal ticket. What had started as a pity job for a struggling law student turned into what should have been understood as a fling. Crooker was so persistent in his pursuit of Norma that she fired him and broke off the relationship.

Even though Crooker had a wife and family, the Pepperdine graduate continued his attempts to woo her back. He had a hard time accepting that she was of a higher social status than he was and that no matter how hard he tried, he was not going to be allowed into that world. Crooker sent her passionate, intellectual love letters, begging her to take him back. However, McCauley shrugged off her ex-lover.

On July 4, 1955, Norma's father, J. A. Thompson, threw a barbecue at his Bel Air home at 773 Stradella Road, but business took him away from his party at the last moment, so Norma stepped in to serve as the hostess. Groomed as a gentle lady, she often stood in for her father at functions that her father could not attend. Family friend John Baird, along with another couple, dropped Norma off at her home at half-past midnight.

The next morning at 7:45, McCauley's five-year-old son Kirk ran to Laura Dromtra, the McCauley's maid, and told her, "Mommy is still asleep!" Dromtra found McCauley's beaten, stabbed, and strangled body on her chaise lounge.

Twenty-one detectives were quickly assigned to the case, but they were not going to be necessary. It seemed Norma had chatted about her houseboy problems to friends and neighbors. Crooker's infatuation with her had frightened Norma.

McCauley had told friends that Crooker was demanding money from her and insinuating that he may talk about some secret that they shared, rumored to be an abortion, which was then against the law.

Crooker was hauled into police headquarters, where he was questioned by Detective Sergeant Jack Hooper and Detective Frank Gravante of the Los Angeles homicide squad for fourteen hours. In those pre-Miranda days, slapping around a suspect in the interrogation room was standard operating procedure. It did not matter that the cops gave Crooker the third degree, because all the evidence already pointed squarely at him. Besides everyone knowing about him and Mrs. McCauley, there were incriminating love letters and Norma's teeth marks on his left hand. Crooker spilled his guts to the police and wrote down his story in detail.

Sneaking into the house, Crooker hid in a closet in Norma's bedroom, waiting for her to come back from the party. According to Crooker, Norma was not shocked to see her former employee in her bedroom, and she remained aloof to his pleas. The final straw was when Norma either fell asleep or feigned sleep while the conversation was taking place. That angered Crooker, who reacted by hitting and choking her. When Norma started to scream, he put his left hand over her mouth and reached into his jacket for his knife. He stabbed her five times in the chest. Norma fought valiantly for her life, biting Crooker's left hand. He grabbed her white lace stole and strangled her with it until she was dead. Seeing her open purse, Crooker took the money that she had in her wallet and then went home and slept.

Despite Crooker's story, it seems more probable that Crooker surprised Norma when he burst out of her closet. She screamed and he started beating her, eventually stabbing and strangling her to death.

Crooker was charged with first degree murder.

On July 7, Crooker's attorney told the press that his client's confession had been coerced. Besides being grilled for fourteen hours nonstop, Crooker claimed that Detective Hooper had punched him in the stomach several times during the interview. He claimed he had written out the confession only with the promise that Detective Gravante would call off Hooper.

The trial began on November 11, 1955, and no one bought Crooker's story. Numerous friends of Norma testified that she was afraid of Crooker and that he tried to blackmail her by informing her parents about their affair. The prosecutor introduced a police report that Norma had filed with the police about Crooker's blackmail attempt. Then there was the confession, and even though it had been beaten out of him, Crooker wrote down information that only an eyewitness could have provided. The jury took only eight hours to deliberate; the verdict was guilty. The judge sentenced Crooker to death.

Crooker fought to appeal the verdict by claiming that he was compelled by the threat of violence to write his confession. The California Court of Appeals ruled that Crooker, a college graduate and student of law, knew that his rights were being violated, yet he still wrote the detailed confession.

On January 10, 1959, California governor Pat Brown commuted Crooker's death sentence. Later, he allowed him to become eligible for parole, which he won in 1972. He married two more times and died in Oregon on November 11, 1992—two marriages and thirty-seven years more than Norma McCauley got.

# Chapter 33

## Firebug

### Stanford Pattan—Glenn County

Stanford Philip Pattan was down on his luck. The twenty-six-year-old married father of three, with another one on the way, could not find a job to support his growing family. With the rent overdue, bills to pay, and an expensive Buick to make payments on, Pattan's wife Portia Lee could not take it any longer. She packed up the kids and moved back to her parents' house until he got his act together.

Permanent work was in short supply during any time of year in western Glenn County, located at the northwest edge of the Sacramento Valley, where the Coastal Mountain Range of eastern Mendocino County comes to a stuttering end of sagebrush and chaparral. The lush Sacramento Valley provides agricultural work, and the wooded foothills supply the lumber for mills, but those are temporary jobs and the few full-time jobs in those areas are reserved for the owners' family members.

During the summertime, the Coastal Mountain Range turns into the beautiful golden hills that California is famous for, but those hills are tinder dry and the slightest spark can create an inferno in a matter of minutes. Most fires are small enough to be contained by full-time crews of the California Department of Forestry and Fire Protection (CDFFP). When confronted with a bigger fire, the CDFFP temporarily hires locals who have had proper firefighting training. The CDFFP also hires support staff to feed and aid the firefighters.

Pattan's father, Phil, was a well-known and well-liked Northern California CDFFP forest fighter, and Stanford, also a trained firefighter, wanted to follow in this father's footsteps; however, he could only get temporary work from the forest service. The brooding Navy veteran came up with a plan to gain employment.

On July 9, 1953, Stanford Pattan drove up into the dry hills near the village of Chrome, threw a lit match into the chaparral, and drove off in his green Buick to the nearby town of Willows. Pattan made sure that he was seen in town. He even went into a bar and had a couple of beers, something that was not a habit for him. He waited for the call to be issued for extra firefighters, but the fire only burned eleven acres and was quickly contained. Angry, he set out to light another fire.

He drove out to Oleta Point and onto Alden Springs Road, ending up at Grindstone Canyon. He got out of his car, fired a couple of rounds from his .22 rifle at nothing, and drove off in low gear, tossing lit matches out of the window. The dry brush quickly ignited and crept through the canyon. Pattan drove to the Forest Service office to sign up for work, but was told that the fire was under control and the only job available that day was for a cook's helper. Pattan took the job.

The fire was easily contained by the fire crews, which included fourteen members of the New Tribes Mission, a nearby Christian seminary that as part of its civil duty to the community provides the forest service with trained firefighting volunteers. By evening, there remained only a few hot spots on Powder House Ridge, on the north side of Grindstone Canyon.

Around ten that evening, on the southeast side of Rattlesnake Ridge at the southern rim of Grindstone Canyon, crews took a dinner break. What they did not know at the moment is that a hot spot had exploded and ran to the northeast and up Rattlesnake Ridge. When the fire reached the top of the ridge, it changed direction and rapidly traveled downslope toward the resting fire fighters. Nine men ran uphill and were spared their lives. Fifteen other men, fourteen of them volunteers from the New Tribes Mission, tried to outrun the fire by fleeing downhill. Unlike in the movies, the men could not outrun the inferno, and they were quickly engulfed by the flames and incinerated.

The freak direction of the fire was caused by the sun-scorched Sacramento Valley cooling off and creating an updraft of warm air. The rushing cooler air from the Coastal Mountains pulled the fire downhill at speeds around seventy miles per hour. The fifteen firefighters did not have a chance to get out of the fire's path.

Stanford Pattan was visibly agitated at the fire base camp, where he served on the chow line. He made excuses about his earlier whereabouts without being asked about it, and he went out of his way to volunteer information, and basically dope-slapped himself after every answer. The police quickly reasoned that Pattan had had something to do with the fire.

Police officers asked Pattan to take them on the route that he had been seen driving the day before, Pattan obliged, digging himself deeper every time he opened his mouth. After the tour, the police went to check on his witnesses. They all agreed that Pattan seemed to know about the fire before anyone else. He was hauled into the Glenn County jail at Willows, where, after a grueling all night interrogation, Pattan admitted his guilt.

"I needed the work and the money," Pattan confessed to the police.

The grand jury refused to indict Pattan on murder charges, as everyone knew that Pattan did not intend to murder his fellow firefighters. He started what is dubbed a "job fire," not an entirely rare occurrence in poor rural areas where employment often depends on calamities.

Pattan plead guilty to two counts of willful burning and received two consecutive terms of one to ten years in San Quentin Prison. He served three years before he was paroled to his hometown of Willows. He quietly lived out the rest of his years in the Sacramento Valley, until he died in 2009. The only thing that the dead firefighters received was a roadside memorial and fifteen concrete crosses on the hillside where they died. Twenty-two children were left without a father.

# Chapter 34

## It's Friday!

### William Liebscher—Fairfax, Marin County

Former United States Air Force pilot William Liebscher wasn't cut out to be a used car dealer. Although at his previous job as a bank teller in San Francisco, he could politely correct any problem a customer might have, he was not prepared for the cutthroat business of automobile sales. When an angry customer came back to him with a car that had quit running properly, he would give the buyer his money back. He was doomed to lose money on his enterprise.

Working out of his Tudor-style home in the elegant Marin County town of Fairfax, Liebscher hustled as much as he could, working all hours of the day and taking many out-of-town trips. His twenty-eight-year-old wife, Jan, had quit her job in the reservations department of an airline after she married William in 1955 and now looked after the home. Their marriage was a happy one; they did not live extravagantly, but they enjoyed the laid-back Marin County lifestyle. William kept Jan out of his business dealings.

On Friday, February 23, 1956, Liebscher used theatrical makeup to make himself look older. Dressed in conservative clothes and looking very inconspicuous, with a fake mustache, he walked into the Anglo California National Bank in San Francisco's Marina District and showed the teller a note asking for twenties, tens, and fives. He was polite and, contrary to popular belief, did not have a gun, real or toy. He got eleven hundred and twenty-five dollars in that robbery and was probably already driving on the Golden Gate Bridge by the time the police showed up at the bank.

The FBI named Liebscher the "Friday Afternoon Bandit" because he always struck just before closing time on Fridays. Although Liebscher didn't know it at the time, he was having the longest successful robbery streak in a long time, and the FBI was using a lot of manpower to try to catch him.

Besides San Francisco, Liebscher hit banks in Daly City, Mountain View, Hayward, Menlo Park, and twice in Los Angeles. Liebscher told Jan that he had to go to Los Angeles on business. She didn't know that it was bank robbing business.

Somewhere along his string of fourteen bank robberies, Liebscher left his stickup note behind with the teller, and a witness got a partial license plate number. The FBI finally had a clue as to who their robber might be.

The police found Liebscher at a Fairfax car lot on July 22, 1957, and he was arrested without incident. Officers were surprised that the unassuming, well-dressed, middle-aged man was the notorious Friday Afternoon Bandit. Liebscher was taken to the Marin County jail in San Rafael and held on a ten thousand–dollar bond.

Liebscher was open with the police and told the agents that he owed several banks money and that after each robbery, he would go to one of the institutions to make payments or to pay off a loan.

"I guess I was too soft as an auto salesman," he told the agents. "When I would sell a used car and someone came back and said the transmission was no good, I felt I had a responsibility to compensate the man. I would make up the loss myself."

A search of the couple's sparsely furnished home revealed nothing. Jan was blindsided by the news that her husband was a bank robber. She took agents to their two safe deposit boxes, but they contained only family papers and the pink slip on their ten-year-old car.

Through his attorney, William told his wife that it would be a good idea to divorce him. Jan, as pragmatic as her husband, asked the press, "Tell me, how can you love a man … how can you consider yourself a realist and live with a man for two years and not know any more about him than this?"

William Liebscher received fifteen years in federal prison and was fined eighty dollars. Jan was at the sentencing and told the press that she had sold everything, gotten a job, and moved into an apartment in San Francisco. After the sentencing, both William and Jan Liebscher dropped out of the public eye.

# Chapter 35

## The Gold Coast Princess

### Karyn Kupcinet—West Hollywood

Roberta Lynn Kupcinet was born on March 6, 1941, to Chicago royalty. Her father, pioneer multimedia personality Irv Kupcinet, was the man that all celebrities visiting Chicago had to call upon. Besides his longtime *Sun-Times* gossip column, "Kup's Column," Kupcinet also had a syndicated television late night talk show that ran from 1959 to 1986. It was not unusual for Roberta to come home from school to find Don Rickles, Phyllis Diller, Sammy Davis, Jr., or Milton Berle cracking jokes with Irv and his brash and foulmouthed wife, Essee.

Growing up in luxury on Chicago's Gold Coast and attending private schools, Roberta, who was known as Cookie when she was a girl, had all the opportunities that a rich, well-connected girl would expect. Essee, an arrogant snob and failed dancer, groomed Cookie for show business. At thirteen, Cookie took up acting and, despite her lack of vocal range, found plenty of work in Chicago theaters.

After high school, Cookie moved to New York to take lessons at the prestigious Actor's Studio. She became obsessed about her weight and appearance. Essee had introduced Cookie to amphetamines, which in 1960 were sold as diet pills and were as easy to get as aspirins. Cookie received extensive plastic surgery to smooth out the little flaws that she and Essee imagined would hold back her acting career.

In 1960, her parents' good friend, comedian Jerry Lewis, offered Cookie a small role in his film, *The Ladies Man*. After moving to Los Angeles and changing her name to Karyn, Kupcinet had little trouble finding parts in television and films. She was the fresh new face in Hollywood and, with her father's connections, she obtained guest roles on *The Donna Reed Show*, *The Red Skelton Show*, and *Hawaiian Eye*.

It was not long before casting directors realized Kupcinet's lack of talent and the acting offers reduced to a trickle by 1962. It was no secret in Hollywood that the starlet had a raging amphetamine addiction that stoked her insecurities and caused irrational behavior. Unlike most young actors in Hollywood, Karyn was supported by a generous allowance provided by her parents. There was nothing that Karyn went without, and she lived at the fashionable Monterey Village apartments at 1227½ Sweetzer Avenue in West Hollywood. Despite her parental safety-net, she was allegedly arrested for shoplifting. Her father's connections made the charges go away.

In 1962, Karyn acted in an episode of the Earl Holliman drama, *The Wide Country*. The short-lived series co-starred Andrew Prine, who had made a splash as Helen Keller's brother in the Academy Award–winning film, *The Miracle Worker*. Karyn and Prine began dating.

Prine had his mind focused on his career and saw Karyn as a casual girlfriend, but Karyn was obsessed with the young actor. Prine quickly tired of Kupcinet's drama queen antics and insecurities and stopped seeing the Gold Coast princess. Karyn responded by cutting random letters out of magazines, like a ransom note, and sending threatening letters to Prine and his estranged wife, actress Sharon Farrell. Kupcinet was also pregnant by Prine, but family friend, actor Mark Goddard, best known as U.S. Space Corps Major Donald West on the television program *Lost In Space*, drove her to Tijuana for an abortion. The overweight, spoiled, whining, clingy, high-maintenance actress was on a trajectory that could only lead to tragedy.

On November 27, 1963, Kupcinet arrived late for dinner at Goddard's home. She was drugged out to the point of drooling, and she told the Goddards that she had found a baby on her doorstep. She went back to her apartment where she watched *The Danny Kaye Show* with actor Robert Hathaway and writer Edwin Stephen Rubin.

Higher than a kite on speed, the restless Kupcinet left the pair to go for a quick walk around the block. After she came back, she served coffee and cake to her guests, and she then excused herself and went to bed. It was not unusual for Karyn to let her guests stay over after she went to bed. Kupcinet had a state-of-the-art television set that her daddy had bought for her, and she was known for her TV parties. Besides, it was Thanksgiving Eve.

Hathaway and Rubin left the apartment around eleven, carefully making sure that the door was locked on their way out. The men went to actor William Mamches' apartment, where they continued to watch television. Andrew Prine showed up, too, and together the four men watched television until three in the morning. Prine told his friends that Kupcinet had called him around midnight and told him about the baby that she claimed to have found on her doorstep, adding that the police had taken the baby away.

On November 30, after not hearing from Karyn since Wednesday evening, Goddard and his wife Marcia drove to the Monterey Village apartments and found the door to her second story apartment unlocked. Walking in, they were immediately hit by the odor of decay. They found the television on, cigarette butts scattered on the floor, along with an empty coffee pot. Karyn was lying facedown and naked on the couch. Body fluids had leaked out of her orifices and maggot eggs were in her hair. She was too decomposed to determine immediately what had caused her death, but the autopsy report listed the cause of death as "murder by manual strangulation." Karyn had a compression fracture on the left side of her hyoid bone, along with deep tissue hemorrhage of the neck. Her thyroid gland, tongue, and larynx were crushed.

The Los Angeles Police Department found Karyn's diary full of insane rantings about her weight, lack of acting work, and Prine. Detectives found threatening notes that were forged by Karyn to make it seem that Prine had sent them. Over ten prescription bottles were found inside her medicine cabinet—mostly uppers and downers.

Prine, Mamches, Hathaway, Rubin, and the Goddards were thoroughly questioned by the police and released. Karyn's downstairs neighbor, David Lange, brother of actress Hope Lange, was also questioned at length. Lange was a known as a chronic alcoholic who often walked into strangers' apartments in a drunken stupor. Lange claimed that he had been out drinking with Natalie Wood and Glenn Ford that night, and he had passed out when he got back to his apartment. A few days later, Lange allegedly joked to friends that he had killed Kupcinet. After that, Lange quit cooperating with the investigators.

The LAPD, pressured by Kupcinet's connections, rushed the investigation by focusing on her entertainment industry friends and not on good, old-fashioned detective work. Despite the best efforts of the LAPD, the murder of Karyn Kupcinet was never solved. Irv Kupcinet went to his grave believing that he knew who murdered his daughter, but the police never had enough evidence to charge anyone.

Six weeks after her murder, Kupcinet appeared on the popular courtroom drama *Perry Mason.* "The Case of the Capering Camera" was Kupcinet's final on-screen appearance.

# Chapter 36

# Shame on You

## Spade Cooley—Willow Springs, Kern County

For a decade, starting in 1941, Spade Cooley was the king of all media, fifty years before Howard Stern. A star of stage, screen, radio, and television, Cooley was known as "the King of Western Swing," a title he won by beating Bob Wills and his Texas Playboys at a battle of the bands held at the Venice Pier Ballroom in 1942.

Born dirt poor in Oklahoma on December 17, 1910, Spade was christened with the improbably Celtic name of Donnell Clyde Cooley. Cooley's father, who was a hoedown fiddler, recognized young Donnell's talent on the violin and made sure that he would be a properly trained musician. Old man Cooley's foresight would serve Donnell well in his career.

In the early 1930s, the Cooley family, as well as thousands of others, fled the Oklahoma Dust Bowl for the bountiful West Coast. Finding himself with a wife and child in Modesto, California, in the early 1930s, Donnell worked menial jobs and played his fiddle at hoedowns and roadhouses up and down Highway 99. He acquired his nickname while playing in Modesto because of his poker skills.

By 1935, Spade realized that he preferred playing music over toiling in the hot and dusty San Joaquin Valley for a few dollars a day. Moving his family to Los Angeles, Spade immediately became an in-demand musician, primarily because he could read music.

Spade struck up a friendship with Roy Rogers while performing with Rogers' former band, The Sons of the Pioneers, and Rogers got him a job as his stand-in/extra at Republic Pictures. At the same time, Spade was playing nights as a sideman with Los Angeles bands.

With the rise of sophisticated Western swing music, a hybrid of hillbilly, bluegrass, and jazz, Cooley put together a crack band of musicians and jumped on the bandwagon. His musicians varied, but generally there were a dozen in the band, plus a female singer. Spade was the quintessential front man, and his musical skills were irrefutable. He and his band dressed to the nines in flashy rhinestone-studded Western suits and cowboy hats. The band performed at the Santa Monica and Venice piers for a year and a half to packed crowds.

Spade Cooley had his first hit with his second single, "Shame on You." It bounced up and down the top-ten charts all through 1945, hitting the number one position nine different times between March and July. Spade rang up five more top-ten hits in the next three years.

When Spade was not performing or handling the business end of his band, he performed in Hollywood Westerns, often with significant roles, as well as a song or three. He eventually appeared in more than fifty films, mostly Westerns and one-reelers.

Spade constantly strove to attract better and hotter musicians for his band. Always a step ahead of the current musical trends, if he could not hire the hottest musician, he hired the next best. He was a kind and generous man when sober, but when in his cups, he was a tyrant. He would fire musicians for an imagined slight, only to beg them to come back after he sobered up. He would turn violent if one of his musicians formed a competing band, especially if the traitor took other members with him. Spade once fired his singer, Tex Williams, on stage in front of a full house. Williams' crime was that he had recently signed as a solo artist with Capitol Records. Most of the members of Spade's band quit in protest and joined Williams in his new band. Spade hired new musicians.

Cooley had a mind for business but a weakness for the ladies. In 1945, he hired twenty-one-year-old Ella Mae Evans to be his singer, even though she was not up to Cooley's high standards. It was not long before Spade divorced Anna, his long-suffering wife.

Nor was it long before the tiny and blonde Ella Mae became pregnant. Her career was over, at Spade's insistence. Their daughter, Melody, was born in 1946, with a brother, Donnell, entering the world in 1948. Believing that his children would have a better life away from Los Angeles, Spade bought a remote ranch north of there, in the Kern County town of Willow Springs. Spade spent most of his time at his Ventura

Boulevard mansion, where he entertained an assortment of female companions.

The future looked as though it would provide endless opportunities for Cooley. In 1946, he had his own popular radio program, *Spade Cooley Time*, on KFVD. The next year, he signed a seven-year lease on the eight thousand–capacity Santa Monica Ballroom. The year 1948 found Spade with a television variety show, *The Hoffman Hayride*, on KTLA-TV. It was the most popular Saturday night television program in the Los Angeles region.

Cooley toured up and down the West Coast performing in shows, with just enough time to make it to his television show and then out to Santa Monica for *The Hoffman Hayride*. Cooley was so popular that it has been alleged that at times he had four different Spade Cooley bands out on the road, complete with Spade Cooley imitators.

By the mid-1950s, the Western swing craze had completely disappeared, and so had Cooley cash cows. He was no longer the clean-looking showman. His television and radio programs were cancelled. The years of whoring, boozing, and pill-popping had turned him into a belligerent, washed-up, middle-aged man. Spade may have been a jerk, but he was worth more than twelve million dollars.

Spade sold his Encino home and moved to his lavish spread in Willow Springs, where he spent much of his time accusing Ella Mae of infidelities. He interrogated her mercilessly and beat her. He was drunk all the time, and his routine of taking uppers to get up and downers to sleep added to his psychosis. He cowed Ella Mae into admitting to whatever twisted sexual fantasy his perverted mind imagined.

Inspired by Disneyland, Spade put together some investors and planned out a Spade Cooley-themed water park, called Water Wonderland. The project was to be built close to Cooley's home in the Tehachapi Mountain foothills; unbeknownst to his investors, much of the land needed for the huge park was owned by one of Cooley's partnerships.

Cooley divided his time between the Water Wonderland project, his various other business interests, his stable of Los Angeles girlfriends (who he had living in nearby motels), and beating the crap out of Ella Mae. Cooley hired a private detective to look into Ella Mae's life—there wasn't much to find, since she lived in the middle of nowhere. Cooley was certain that she had been unfaithful to him while he was in Los Angeles performing on stage and screen.

Ella Mae finally had a nervous breakdown, sent her children to live with relatives, and checked into a sanitarium to rest. Despite his wife's delicate position, Spade did not let up on his mistrust, even though his private detective could find no evidence that Ella Mae was ever unfaithful to him.

After Ella Mae recovered somewhat, she returned to the ranch, where she was virtually held prisoner, suffering more beatings and interrogations by Spade. Daughter Melody overheard Spade telling someone on the telephone, "In six months, we'll be married." She tried to get her mother to leave, but Ella Mae was too weak to drive her car. Spade tried to get Ella Mae to go for a ride with him, but she was terrified of the man and became hysterical. Allegedly, Spade had once tried to push her out of his moving car. Ella Mae was a shell of a human being.

On April 3, 1961, Spade was drunk and irritable at a Water Wonderland meeting with his investors. He left abruptly and angrily. Nobody knows exactly when Spade beat Ella Mae to death, but she was dead in the late afternoon when Melody came home from a friend's house.

When Melody arrived home, Spade was on the telephone, and Melody saw that her father was sweaty, with spots of blood on his clothing. She heard him tell the person on the other end of the line not to call police; he then hung up quickly and asked her to talk to her mother. He dragged the teenager into a bathroom, located off the den and showed her Ella Mae's bruised and bloody body lying naked in the shower. Spade grabbed Ella Mae by her hair and dragged her limp body into the den, pulling Melody along with him while calling his dead wife a slut and other obscenities.

Spade asked Melody if she thought Ella Mae was dead and then stomped his wife hard several times with his cowboy boots. He then put out his lit cigarette on her dead body, pulled out a gun, and asked Melody if she wanted to die. Suddenly, the telephone rang, distracting the inebriated King of Western Swing long enough for the young woman to run out of the house.

The police were not called until after ten that evening and the cops didn't arrive till around eleven. Spade's manager, a family friend, and Spade's adult son from his first marriage, along with his son's wife, all waited with Spade for the police.

Cooley was arrested and taken to the Kern County jail, sixty-three miles away in Bakersfield.

All of the positive things that Spade had done for California's large Okie population through his music and persona were undone. The negative stereotype of Okies being incorrigible, brutal, drunken hicks was proven once again, and by their most celebrated son. Spade received no love from his old fans.

Cooley also found zero support among Los Angeles musicians and media. He had burnt all of his bridges when he was on top. His reputation of violent behavior and womanizing left no doubt in the minds of most of his former associates that he was very capable of murder.

Bakersfield in the early 1960s was one of the hottest musical locations for country music. Dust Bowl refugees Buck Owens and Merle Haggard, the leaders of the hard-driving, rock 'n' roll–influenced country sound, stayed away from Cooley as if he were the plague.

Cooley pleaded not guilty by reason of insanity, and he made sure his trial was as dramatic as his alcohol-soaked mind would allow. Fainting spells, tears, and an alleged heart attack helped make his thirty-day trial the longest in Kern County history.

The evidence was overwhelming. Kern County district attorney Kit Nelson accused Cooley of murder by torture, and, with the aid of the Los Angeles Sheriff's Department, made a very strong case. Forensic expert Clifford Cromp pointed out that Ella Mae's body had old bruises, as well as new ones. She had numerous cigarette burns on her in different stages of healing. Her genitals were badly bruised, and a broomstick found in the home had traces of hair, blood, and vaginal and fecal matter on it.

It was daughter Melody's testimony that sealed Cooley's fate. The fourteen-year-old bravely took the witness stand to tell the jury about life at the Cooley ranch. She told of Spade's drunken behavior, gunplay, threats, and the beatings that he gave Ella Mae. Her story could not be shaken by the attorneys for the defense.

Cooley didn't make things any better for himself when he took the witness stand and denied everything. He stuck to his story that Ella Mae had fallen out of his moving car a few days before and that he had found her unconscious in the shower. He denied stomping his wife in front of his daughter and using her as an ashtray. He could not explain his bruised fingers and hands when he was booked into jail. Fiddlers are generally very careful with their hands.

Cooley rambled off-topic and told the jury that his wife was part of a sex cult and that at one time during their marriage she had had an affair with Cooley's friend and neighbor, actor Roy Rogers. An angry Rogers categorically denied the affair and told the press that he had never even been to the Cooley ranch without Cooley being present.

The jury came back with a guilty verdict, and Cooley withdrew his insanity plea. Judge William Bradshaw sentenced the King of Western Swing to life in prison. Due to Spade's delicate health, he was sent to the California State Medical Facility at Vacaville rather than to notorious Folsom or San Quentin prisons.

While in prison, Cooley found God, was a model prisoner, and played in a prison band. Governor Ronald Reagan, a former B-actor who had surely rubbed elbows with Spade during their Hollywood days, made the parole board aware that he wanted to see Cooley paroled. The parole board agreed, and Spade was set to be released on his sixtieth birthday, February 22, 1970.

But Cooley did not live to be a free man. On November 23, 1969, Cooley was given a seventy-two-hour furlough to perform at the Oakland Auditorium for a benefit for the Deputy Sheriffs' Association of Alameda County. Moments after he left the stage to a standing ovation, while signing autographs backstage, Spade suffered a massive heart attack. Prophetically, his final song of the night was "It's Time to Live, It's Time to Die." He wrote the song while in prison.

# Chapter 37

## Fleecing the Flock

### C. Thomas Patten—Oakland

Carl Thomas Patten was born in Tennessee, where his father was a bootlegger who was often in trouble with the law. The apple does not fall far from the tree and the younger Patten, who bragged that the "C." stood for "Cash," ran scams, cons, and other criminal activity. In 1935, Patten was arrested for transporting stolen automobiles across state lines.

Patten slipped through the jaws of justice and later that year married twenty-two-year-old Wilma "Bebe" Harrison, who had been an evangelical preacher since the age of seventeen. Together, they toured America, preaching in revival style out of their car and collecting whatever money they could squeeze out of the migrant workers and rural bumpkins who came to hear the word of the Lord.

Making their way to Southern California, the Pattens landed on the stairs of Aimee Semple McPherson's Four Square Church. McPherson's popularity had been tarnished by her 1926 false kidnapping and sex scandal; however, that did not stop her true believers, who continued to donate heavily to her church. The couple learned at the knee of McPherson, and they began to wear flowing robes, to use radio to broadcast their services, and to accept nonwhites and non-Christians into their flock. They also learned how to separate their congregation from its money.

After learning all of the Reverend McPherson's tricks, the couple drove north in 1944 to set up camp in Oakland, which was bursting at its seams as uneducated Okies, southern whites, and African Americans moved there to work for the war effort. Towns like Richmond and Vallejo became cities overnight, as Henry Kaiser's shipyard produced at full capacity, launching a ship a day.

Using paid advertisements on the radio and in the newspapers, Bebe Patten's preaching started to attract multitudes of weak-minded and gullible people. For anyone who did not have a radio or was illiterate, mobile loudspeakers on trucks drove through East Bay neighborhoods, advertising salvation at Bebe's satin shoes. Money rolled in from the sold-out revival shows at Oakland's Elm Tabernacle. Bebe and Cash went on to rent the larger Oakland Women's City Club. When that space became too small, they rented the eight thousand-seat Oakland Arena.

Cash spent the church donations on two hundred pairs of custom made cowboy boots, nine luxury automobiles, and a cabin cruiser. The chubby-faced con man had a fondness for loud shirts and cowboy suits. While Bebe preached about salvation, Cash worked the crowd, literally shaking down the congregation, physically threatening them with God's wrath if they did not give more money.

Cash was an experienced con-artist and he knew well how to get everything he could while the pickings were hot. He persuaded some of his followers to write the church into their wills, turn over stocks and bonds, sign over promissory notes, and give the Pattens control over their worldly possessions.

Later in 1944, the Pattens came up with another scam. They opened the Oakland Bible Institute at 1428 Alice Street in downtown Oakland and claimed that it was accredited by the University of California. Bebe, who bought a Ph.D. from a diploma mill, became the school's president. Eventually, the Pattens would own four corporations: The Oakland Bible Church, the Oakland Bible Institute, Patten College and Seminary, and the Patten Foundation. In two short years, Bebe and Carl went from selling their car's spare tire to buy soup to being millionaires.

The Pattens had looked to 1950 as a banner year as the money kept pouring into their various foundations and schools, but cracks were forming in their scam. Money was supposed to go to church-run projects like a Lake County orphanage and a new temple, neither of which was ever built. Gordon Hagglund, a 1947 graduate of Patten Seminary, went to the Contra Costa County district attorney and told him of the Pattens' scam.

Bebe and Carl were indicted on ten counts of misuse of $20,670 of congregation money. The trial came to order on February 20, 1950, just three weeks after Bebe gave birth to twin daughters. Somehow, the charges of aiding and abetting against Bebe were dropped. Cash was taking the fall.

Costa Contra County judge Charles Wade Snook presided, with Richard Chamberlain and Cecil Mosbacher working as assistant district attorneys. Mosbacher would go on to become the first female judge in Contra Costa County history. The Pattens had four attorneys. The courtroom was cleared on the first day, as the Pattens' followers crowded the courtroom, creating disturbances and shouting "amen."

The prosecution exposed the Pattens as common flimflam artists who never paid their bills, bullied and tricked their worshipers out of their money, and used their church funds in complicated real estate deals. If Patten would have stopped there, he probably would have gotten away with his con, but the old huckster could not leave a rube alone once he spotted one.

Freeda Borchardt loaned the church almost $8,000. The fifty-two-year-old Borchardt told the court that she had given Patten the money in three different transactions. Gussa Norton gave Patten a $4,000 inheritance check to cash, from which she was to give him a $400 bequest. Patten gave her $232 back and an IOU for the rest of the money. Shipyard worker Elof Hagglund was taken for $4,000, and barber Gustav Rode was bilked out of $2,500. George and May Lewis loaned Patten $3,000 to help buy the City Club Hotel. They had sold their West Virginia property to help out the pastor.

The preachers were accused of raising $30,000, supposedly to make a deposit for a radio station license. An agent from the Federal Communication Commission testified that the FCC does not require a deposit for a broadcasting license.

The Pattens were portrayed as greedy intimidators who were not beyond shaming the accusers from the pulpit. Carl blatantly wore fancy clothes, drove expensive cars, and often bragged about how he was twice a millionaire. The couple had multiple bank accounts and a twisted web of bad loans and bounced checks. The religious leader bounced two checks for a total of $4,200 at the Palace Club, a Reno gambling establishment.

Bebe, who had a fondness for silk gowns and fox furs, had a penchant for not paying her designers.

During the trial, students from Patten College loudly protested outside. The defense presented nineteen witnesses. They were all hazy about what they remembered and were thoroughly discredited by the prosecution. At one point in the proceedings, Carl suffered a heart attack and spent the rest of the trial at an Oakland hospital. He arrived in court to hear the verdict wearing silk pajamas, cared for by uniformed nurses. He was found guilty of grand theft and sentenced to five to fifty years in San Quentin Prison, just across the San Francisco Bay.

Carl Thomas Patten was released from prison after three years. Under the conditions of his parole, he was banned from any business involving Bebe's church. The old con man knew when the con was over and lived the rest of his life in luxury, behind closed gates, until he died of a heart attack on May 12, 1958.

Bebe went on to great heights as an evangelist. She received numerous awards and honors, and she became an avid supporter of Israel. Her daily thirty-minute radio broadcast, *The Shepherd Hour*, aired from 1951 to 1987. Her television program, *The Bebe Patten Hour*, was aired from 1976 to 2004. Her periodical, *The Trumpet Call*, is still being published. Bebe died on January 25, 2004, at the age of ninety-one.

# Chapter 38
# The Ruler
## John "Bunny" Breckenridge—San Francisco/Los Angeles

John "Bunny" Breckenridge was born with a silver spoon in his mouth in Paris, France, on August 6, 1903. An heir of former Senator William Sharon, initial investor of the Comstock Lode mine in Nevada, and the same William Sharon who was entangled with David Terry, Mary Ellen Pleasant, and Sarah Althea Hill (see Chapter 4, "Psycho Politician," and Chapter 6, "Voodoo Queen"), Breckenridge grew up in France and England. Allegedly educated at Eton and Oxford, Bunny reveled in the life of the filthy rich. After school, the great-grandson of decorated Confederate general and U.S. vice president John C. Breckenridge moved to Paris, where he acted in drag revues. In 1927, he married and impregnated a member of French nobility, but the marriage lasted only two years. Moving back to London, Bunny acted in Shakespearean theater. Breckenridge spoke with an effeminate intonation, so hearing him recite Shakespeare must have hilarious.

Moving to San Francisco in the late 1920s, Bunny carried on his life of debauchery and excess. He was an openly gay man during a time when it was dangerous to declare such things, even in San Francisco. He wore heavy eyeliner, dressed outrageously in silks and gaudy costume jewelry, and threw extravagant parties at his San Francisco home.

Somehow, Breckenridge stayed under the radar during the thirties and forties, despite his outrageous attire, makeup, and flamboyantly lecherous manner. Breckenridge hired only good-looking, young male bodybuilders to work for him as cooks, valets, chauffeurs, and bodyguards. In 1954, he blew the top off his quiet life of self-indulgence when he announced that he planned on moving to Denmark, so he could undergo a sex-change operation and marry his boyfriend. At the same time, his blind and elderly mother sued him from England for nonpayment of promised support. The judge ordered Bunny to pay his mother an eight thousand-dollar-a-year stipend.

## Gay San Francisco

One of the reason San Francisco became known as a gay-friendly city is because of the presence of the United States Navy. Sailors who were caught in a homosexual act overseas were given dishonorable discharges when they got to port in one of the many San Francisco Bay bases. Instead of going back to Runnells, Iowa, and explaining to Ma and Pa how they got booted out of the navy, many men decided to stay in San Francisco.

In 1955, homosexuality was illegal in San Francisco, and homosexuals caught soliciting sex or in other compromising situations were charged with vagrancy. After being arrested for vagrancy in a waterfront bar in San Francisco, Bunny decided to have his sex change in Mexico. However, his sex change plans got put on hold after he was injured in a serious car crash.

Despite his wealth, Bunny spent part of 1958 loafing in Southern California as a houseguest of actor Paul Marco, a Los Angeles native and a member of director Ed Wood's troupe of bad actors. At the time, Wood was working on his greatest project, *Plan 9 from Outer Space*, and Marco had the role of Officer Kelton, the dim-witted police officer in the graveyard. When Wood needed an actor to play the Ruler, an alien supervillain meant to instill fear among film viewers, he naturally asked the lascivious, Shakespearean-trained, effeminate drag queen John Breckenridge if he would like the part.

Bunny dove into the role with the same flair he displayed in his everyday life. Wearing a chiffon blouse with slightly puffy sleeves under a long, black sleeveless sweater—complete with a shield symbol behind a claymore ax on the chest—and black trousers tucked into light-colored suede boots, Bunny did not exactly look like a feared leader. Bunny's acting ability ranged from rolling his heavily made-up eyes to appearing uninterested. Not bothering to learn his lines, Bunny read off cue cards and notes at a World War II surplus desk littered with surplus electronic gear. Wood shot the scene with uncharacteristic skill, utilizing cutaway editing and a slow zoom out. Although Bunny was on screen for less than five minutes, his scene was key to the plot, as Bunny portrayed the leader of the invading aliens and gave the order to raise an army of the dead to take over Earth. Instead of invoking fear, his performance brought howls of laughter from the audience. It was Bunny's only film.

Back in northern California, Breckenridge lazed with the idle rich of the Monterrey Peninsula. In an act of extremely bad judgment, a female friend left her ten- and twelve-year-old boys in Bunny's care while she vacationed at Lake Tahoe. Growing bored, Bunny took the boys on a trip that they no doubt never forgot.

After showing the brothers Las Vegas, they drove to Hollywood. There the story gets murky, but the gist is that the boys were caught soliciting sex from an undercover police officer. While the boys were not exactly Boy Scouts, Breckenridge was responsible for their well-being while their mother partied in Tahoe.

Bunny was arrested while registering at a luxurious Beverly Hills hotel, along with accomplices Cecil Mahaffy, Thomas Jordan, and Ross Willson, all young men in their twenties. Breckenridge hired attorney to the stars Jerry Giesler, who had represented such Hollywood rogues as Charlie Chaplin, Robert Mitchum, Errol Flynn, and mobster Bugsy Siegel. Giesler managed to get the court to sentence Bunny to three months at the Atascadero State Hospital because he was potentially dangerous to himself. The boys' father filed a $3 million lawsuit against Breckenridge for neglecting his children.

Once Bunny was released, he kept a lower profile for the rest of his long life. He entertained guests in his home in Carmel-by-the-Sea, where he acted in local theater productions and relished his cult status brought on by late night viewings of *Plan 9 from Outer Space.*

Bunny died on November 5, 1995, in Carmel. He was the longest living cast member of *Plan 9 from Outer Space.*

# Chapter 39

## The Sacramento Vampire

### Richard Trenton Chase—Sacramento

It is an understatement to say that Richard Trenton Chase was insane. Born on May 23, 1950, to a dysfunctional family, Chase tortured small animals and set fires as a child. He was killing cats by the time he was ten years old. As a teenage stoner and drinker, Chase had trouble getting erections whenever he got lucky with women he knew.

Chase went to a psychiatrist, who told him that repressed anger was the cause of his impotence. The psychiatrist also believed that he had more serious problems, but Chase stopped going to his appointments.

Chase's revolving door of roommates all thought he was a bizarre person and a heavy drug user. He once nailed his closet door shut because he believed that someone was living inside. A hypochondriac, Chase believed that his stomach was backwards, that bones were coming out of the back of his head, and that someone had stolen his pulmonary artery.

Chase's mother convinced him to see another psychiatrist, who diagnosed the six foot-tall, one hundred and forty-pound man as a paranoid schizophrenic with drug-induced toxic psychosis. The good doctor had no idea how correct his diagnosis was.

Completely drugged out of his mind, Chase began to kill and disembowel rabbits, both domesticated and wild. He ate their entrails raw. Sometimes, he used a blender to liquefy the animals so that he could drink them down like a milkshake. Eventually, he began to intravenously inject rabbit blood, which resulted in a bad case of blood poisoning and a stay in a mental hospital.

The doctors believed that Chase's problems were caused by drug abuse. In 1976, he escaped for a short time and used his freedom to kill two birds and drink their blood. Not long after his escape, the doctors decided that Chase was no longer a threat.

With his mother as guardian, Chase was released into society. She paid his rent and shopped for his groceries. Chase fell through the holes in the social safety net and back into his old habits. He went off his medications and resumed killing small animals in order to drink their blood. He took one more ominous step: He purchased a handgun.

Ambrose Griffin was unloading groceries from the family car on December 29, 1977, when he started screaming. His wife ran outside and, seeing him prostrate, believed he had had a heart attack. He had been randomly shot by Chase. A few days before, police had collected bullets from the wall of a Sacramento home that had been randomly shot up. They checked them against the bullet that had killed Griffin and discovered they were from the same gun.

Chase began to break into people's homes, stealing valuables and sometimes urinating or defecating on the furniture. In Chase's twisted mind, if a door was unlocked, it was an invitation to enter the premises.

On January 23, 1978, Chase entered the home of twenty-two-year-old Teresa Wallin. Chase shot Wallin, who was three months pregnant, twice in the head and once in the arm. He then dragged the dying woman into her bedroom.

Wallin's husband found his wife's bloody body when he came home from work later that night. The gruesome crime scene made seasoned policemen sick. Wallin's clothes were pulled over her head and ankles. Her left nipple was cut off and her chest and abdomen were splayed open. Her spleen and intestines were pulled out. Although she was already dead, she had been stabbed multiple times. Her pancreas was cut in two, and her kidneys had been cut out and placed back inside her body. There was evidence that Chase had drunk Wallin's blood from a discarded yogurt cup.

Four days later and a mile from the Wallin crime scene, Chase struck again. Entering Evelyn Miroth's home, he murdered her, her visiting friend, Dan Meredith, her six-year-old son, Jason, and her twenty-month-old nephew, David.

Neighbors discovered the gory site the next day. Meredith was found in the hallway, shot in the head. Jason was found in his bedroom, shot twice in the head. Evelyn had been mutilated, her intestines thrown around her bedroom. She also had been sexually assaulted and sexually mutilated. There was no sign of young David, only a blood-spattered crib. Meredith's car was also missing.

Investigators theorized that David was killed in his crib and brought into the bathroom, where Chase cracked open his skull, spilling his brains into the bathtub. The police matched the bloody footprints to the ones found at the Wallin murder. Witnesses came forward to tell police that a young, skinny man was in the neighborhood that day, asking for old magazines.

With a madman on the loose, Sacramento police and the FBI canvassed homes and businesses in the neighborhood, figuring that since the crimes happened in the same area, the killer would eventually be identified. After getting information from the gun store where Chase purchased his .22 caliber pistol, the police raided Chase's Watt Avenue apartment.

The police found Chase in his bloodstained apartment. A gore-covered blender contained small pieces of bone. In the refrigerator, detectives found a container of brains. A calendar on the wall had the dates of the Wallin and Miroth murders circled and notated with the word "today." There were forty-four more days circled in the months ahead. Meredith's wallet was found on Chase, but the young child was not in the apartment. Chase was tossed in jail.

On March 24, 1977, a janitor from the Arcade Wesleyan Church found Miroth's nephew David's decapitated body in a cardboard box behind the church. His broken, mummified body showed signs of stabbing. His head was found under his body, a bullet hole between his eyes. The keys to Meredith's car were also found in the box.

Chase was charged with six counts of first degree murder. Because of the pretrial publicity in Sacramento, the trial was moved to Santa Clara County. The proceedings began on January 2, 1979, and ended on May 8, 1979, and after five hours of deliberation, the jury found Chase guilty on all counts. He was sentenced to death in San Quentin's gas chamber.

Not a popular inmate, even on death row, Chase was badgered by the other inmates and encouraged to kill himself. On December 26, 1980, guards found Chase dead in his cell. He had taken an overdose of the prescription drug Sinequan after hording the pills for that purpose.

There was one less vampire in California.

# Chapter 40

## The Grifter

### Dorothea Puente—Sacramento

Despite her Hispanic surname, Dorothea Puente was born Dorothea Helen Gray on January 9, 1929, in the San Bernardino County town of Redlands. Dorothea's father, Jesse James Gray, a World War I veteran, was originally from Missouri. His lungs were damaged from a gas attack on the front lines in France, and he was a frail and sickly man. Puente's mother, Trudy Mae Gates, hailed from Oklahoma and was a promiscuous drunkard who ran with a tough crowd. Allegedly, Trudy was a part-time prostitute. She was rarely home, and when she was, she argued incessantly with Jesse. Dorothea was the sixth of seven children born into this hellhole.

Sometime during the 1930s, the Gray family moved to Los Angeles so that Jesse could be closer to the veterans' hospitals. His condition turned into tuberculosis and he had no hope of getting better. Trudy spent more time at the Los Angeles County jail than she did at home. Jesse died in 1937, and Trudy lost custody of her children the next year. The children were all placed in an orphanage. By the end of 1938, Trudy had died in a motorcycle accident and Dorothea and her siblings were orphans.

Dorothea coped with her sad and lonely childhood by telling tall tales and outright lies about her life. By the time she was sixteen years old, Dorothea was working as a prostitute in Olympia, Washington. She met her first husband, a soldier, while working at a cathouse there. But married life bored Dorothea. She drank alcohol and told stories about hobnobbing with movie stars and being in Hiroshima when the atomic bomb was dropped on the city. She left her husband for long periods of time, yet managed to give birth to two daughters between 1946 and 1948. Relatives raised her first daughter; her second daughter was put up for adoption.

Dorothea went on to marry three other men and decided to keep her third husband's surname, Puente. She stole checks and prostituted herself to make ends meet. An occasional stint in jail was just part of the cost of doing business. Because Puente was incapable of telling the truth, she always took a plea bargain to avoid cross-examination.

By the time Puente was thirty years old, she was overweight and looked twice her age. In the early 1960s, Dorothea started a bordello under the guise of a bookkeeping firm in a rented storefront in Sacramento. Her house of ill-repute charged the odd sum of $7.50 for oral sex. The place was eventually raided, and Dorothea pleaded no contest, as she always did.

In the late 1960s, Puente finally found a real job, working at an outpatient home for alcoholics. She used that experience to start her own home for the indigent and addicted, except that she would take, with or without their consent, their Social Security and government assistance checks. If they complained, she'd toss them out of the home and call the police.

Puente took her tenants' money and bought beautiful and fashionable outfits to wear. Her hair was always done in a neat and conservative updo, and she donned expensive jewelry and perfume. She generously donated money to charities and political campaigns. It was part of her fantasy to be an important person. Her compulsive lying helped her considerably. She told anyone who would listen that she was a former model, doctor, or lawyer. The poor orphan had climbed up out of her hellhole and made good.

Puente now looked like a harmless elderly grandmother, but it was a façade. She drank alcohol to excess, but hated drunken people. She wouldn't hesitate to punch out an inebriated tenant before she tossed him down the front stairs.

After one of Puente's alcoholic tenants was incarcerated and didn't receive his social security checks while in jail, he started making inquires. He soon discovered that his signature had been forged. An investigation was initiated and Puente lost her business, her social standing, and her income.

Ever resourceful, Puente started a catering business with a tenant, Ruth Munroe. She also padded her income by dressing up as a nurse and sneaking into hospitals to steal patients' belongings. Another of her scams was to dope the drinks of unsuspecting friends and casual bar pickups and then steal their money, checks, drugs, and jewelry while they were unconscious. She was eventually arrested for this pattern of crimes.

At the time of Puente's arrest, Ruth Munroe took ill and died. The police suspected that Puente had killed her, but lacked the evidence to charge her. Puente was sentenced to five years at the California Institute for Women at Frontera. She was paroled after two and a half years.

Next, Puente started an unlicensed boardinghouse for the elderly, infirm, and alcoholic at 1426 F Street in Sacramento's Alkali Flats neighborhood. Once again, she quickly got control of her tenants' Social Security and federal assistance checks. This time, she was determined to keep her scheme a secret. When her tenants became too sick or troublesome, she'd spike their food with the sedative Dalmane. After letting them fall into unconsciousness, she would smother them with a pillow. She would bury them in her backyard and continue cashing their benefit checks. Eventually, she had murdered Alvaro Montoya, James Gallop, Ben Fink, Dorothy Miller, Vera Faye Martin, Everson Gillmouth, Leona Carpenter, and Betty Palmer. For some unknown reason, Puente buried Palmer in the front yard, having severed Palmer's head, arms, and feet so that she wouldn't have to dig too deep. Gillmouth was put into a makeshift coffin and dumped by her handyman on the banks of the Sacramento River.

After many relatives and case workers reported missing people whose last address was 1426 F Street, the police swooped down on the house. While they were digging up bodies from her yard, Puente charmed a police detective into allowing her to go around the corner to get a cup of coffee. She promptly got on a bus to Los Angeles, much to the embarrassment of the Sacramento Police Department. She was caught a few weeks later in Los Angeles when a man that Puente was seducing saw her photo on the television news.

After a grueling three-year trial, Puente was convicted of only three counts of murder and was sentenced to life in prison. She died of natural causes on March 27, 2011, at the Central California Women's Facility (CCWF) in Chowchilla. She maintained her innocence all the way to her deathbed.

# Chapter 41

## Taxed Out

### Jim Ray Holloway—Sacramento

Jim Ray Holloway was a troubled man. Born in 1939, the former California Highway Patrol officer had a career filled with transfers, from East Los Angeles to Tracy and, eventually, to Stockton, where he voluntarily resigned in 1972 to take a job with the California Department of Alcoholic Beverage Control. His career with the ABC was filled with accusations of inefficiency, inexcusable neglect of duty, dishonesty, filing of false reports, inexcusable absences without leave, and discourteous treatment of the public and fellow employees.

In March 1984, a drunken Holloway terrorized fellow campers at Coyote Lake Park, a Santa Clara County park near Gilmore, by acting in an obnoxious and threatening manner. He passed out his ABC business card to two campers and talked about the weapons he had with him. Holloway was officially sanctioned by the ABC and resigned in August 1985.

After his wife died in 1990, Holloway moved from Milpitas to the San Joaquin County town of Manteca, where he kept a low profile. Then, in March 1993, Holloway received a sixteen hundred-dollar tax bill and hit the ceiling. He spent a few days staking out the State Board of Equalization building in Sacramento, making mental notes of the structure.

On March 26, 1993, Holloway made his move. He walked into the state office and showed his old badge to a guard, Bruce Broome, but Broome knew that something was not right with Holloway and would not let him get past the lobby. Holloway returned to his blue Ford Econoline van and sat inside for a few minutes to think things over.

At approximately ten in the morning, Holloway, armed with a 12-gauge shotgun, a lever-action .30-30 rifle, a .45 caliber pistol, rope, flares, and two hundred rounds of ammunition, walked back into the building and confronted the guard who had just denied him access. Holloway disarmed the guard, took him outside, and handcuffed him to a parking meter.

Holloway entered the foyer and fired his shotgun four times into the guard's desk. Other guards had seen Holloway cuff their fellow worker outside and called the Sacramento Police Department. In the meantime, Broome freed himself from the parking meter and returned to the building, and he was right behind Holloway when the shooting began.

Holloway grabbed anyone within reach and took him or her hostage. He got into an express elevator and went to the eighteenth floor. Holloway had a list of people he wanted to kill, but he found himself in the wrong building, and none of the people on his hit list were there. He walked around the floor, letting the fleeing employees run for their lives. He wasn't interested in general mayhem; he was searching for certain employees who were in a different building, blocks away.

As hundreds of people fled the building, Sacramento's SWAT team entered and went into action. At 10:30 a.m., a five-member team arrived on the eighteenth floor and immediately confronted Holloway at the end of a hallway, but the angry citizen said that he wouldn't be taken alive.

The SWAT team fired between nine and seventeen rounds from their MP5 submachine guns. One hit Holloway in the face and he fell back into an office cubicle. As Sergeant Patrick Dowden approached the bleeding man, Holloway started to rise, leveling a half-cocked rifle at the officer. Sergeant Dowden commanded Holloway to drop the gun, but Holloway refused and Dowden shot him nine times. Holloway died forty minutes later.

# Chapter 42

## Savannah Smiled?

### Shannon Wilsey—Los Angeles

Shannon Michelle Wilsey was born on October 9, 1970, in Mission Viejo, California, and she was raised in Texas and Southern California. She grew into a wholesome-looking, beautiful young woman with a penchant for rock musicians and hard drugs. A loner super groupie who slept with rock's royalty, she would become known to the world as the beautiful blonde porn star Savannah.

Shannon liked being around the wild rock scene of Hollywood and liked the wild rock 'n' roll men even better. She moved in with Gregg Allman, singer and keyboardist for the legendary southern rock group The Allman Brothers Band when she was nineteen years old. Allman, a notorious drug user himself, kicked Shannon out of his house two years later, allegedly because of her drug use. Their twenty-three-year age difference probably added to the strain of the relationship.

Allman introduced Shannon to the elite Los Angeles party scene, where there was always a silver bowl of grade A cocaine nearby, a never-ending supply of booze, and crazy sexcapades out in the open, like in a barnyard. Shannon had affairs with high-profile rock stars like Axl Rose and Slash of Guns N' Roses, Mötley Crüe front man Vince Neil, Van Halen singer David Lee Roth, punk rocker Billy Idol, and rapper-turned actor-Mark Wahlberg.

Without her sugar daddy Allman, Shannon found herself in need of money. She first posed naked for a magazine and soon afterward signed an exclusive contract with pornographic film company Vivid Entertainment. Shannon took the stage name Savannah, after her favorite film, *Savannah Smiles*. A natural blonde with flawless features, she is considered to have been one of the most beautiful women in porn. Between 1991 and 1994, she performed in more than eighty pornographic films.

With her newfound stardom, Savannah became a demanding diva on the set, often arriving late or failing to show up for shoots. She often showed up wasted, delaying the shoot and costing the producers money. Performance-wise, she was known as a cold fish who put little effort into her "acting." One inside joke among the male performers was that the best thing about screwing Savannah was when the director called "Cut!" As Savannah's fame grew, she made quips and comments about her rock star conquests to the press. She assigned their lovemaking skills a rating from one to ten, and she discussed their various likes and dislikes. This embarrassed more than a few macho rock stars.

Savannah's ego and heroin use got the best of her, and she was fired from Vivid Entertainment. With her reputation preceding her, she found that the industry was not interested in her anymore. A rejection from Hustler magazine for a photo spread damaged her heroin-saturated sense of self-worth. Around this time, her boyfriend, comedian Pauly Shore, broke up with her over her cocaine and heroin addiction.

Depressed, heartbroken, and owing the Internal Revenue Service back taxes, Savannah was booked into a high-paying exotic dancing show at a gentlemen's club in New York by her manager, Nancy Pera. Such a lucrative gig was just what she needed to help pay off the IRS.

On July 11, 1991, a few hours before she was to leave for New York, a loaded Savannah crashed her Corvette near her rented home in the Hollywood Hills. Her face was cut and bleeding and she had broken her nose.

Savannah telephoned Pera and hysterically told her what had happened. Her East Coast show would have to be canceled, and she would lose the desperately needed income. Even more terrifying to her, she would need plastic surgery for her damaged face, with no guarantee that she would be the same again. Pera told her that she would be over to see Savannah in minutes.

Pera arrived at the home at 3802 Multiview Drive in Universal City, only to find the police and EMTs already there. A friend had found Savannah lying in the garage, bleeding from a bullet wound to the head, and called for an ambulance. Savannah apparently missed shooting herself in the temple, hitting the top of her skull instead. She was put on life support for several hours before her estranged father allowed doctors to pull the plug on her.

Fewer than fifty people attended her funeral.

# Chapter 43

## The Naked Guy

### Andrew Martinez—Berkeley

Growing up in Cupertino, Andrew Martinez was a polite, popular, and athletic young man. He was a straight A student and played defensive lineman at Monta Vista High School. When he was seventeen, he decided that clothing was a form of repression and determined to become a nudist. Ever the considerate person, Martinez first went door-to-door in his neighborhood to ask neighbors if they had any objections to his nudity.

Wearing only a backpack and sandals, Martinez got about a mile from his home when a police officer stopped him. Putting that experiment behind him, Martinez enrolled at the University of California, Berkeley, in 1991 to study business and sociology.

During his second year at Berkeley, Martinez started showing up for class in the buff. He always put a sweatshirt on the seat of his chair, and if someone objected, he would put on some clothing. The six-foot, two-inch-tall student, with handsome looks and a toned body, was a member of Berkeley's judo team. Martinez was always candid and straightforward about his nudity, saying that he was challenging the sexual repression of Western society.

The city of Berkeley is known throughout the world as the fountainhead of freethinkers and radical intellectuals, so it was no surprise that the gentle and charismatic Martinez inspired a political movement. In September 1992, Martinez organized several "nude-ins" around Berkeley and San Francisco, some that attracted ten thousand people, although only a couple of dozen were naked. Martinez appeared in the buff on the national television talk shows *The Montel Williams Show* and *The Maury Povich Show*, and he wrote an editorial explaining his nudity for the *Oakland Tribune*.

In the fall of 1992, Martinez was arrested for indecent exposure while jogging, but his novel ideology got the charges dropped. He was arrested soon afterward, again for indecent exposure, when he showed up for his court appearance naked.

The UC Berkeley administration passed an anti-nudity law as part of the Student Code of Conduct, and Martinez was quickly expelled. Not being in school or having a job, and knowing that his fifteen minutes of fame were up, the "Naked Guy," as he had become known, felt betrayed by his supporters as they all went on with their lives. He didn't have the money to file a lawsuit against the giant UC system, and nobody offered to help him. You could say that he felt naked.

Martinez hung out in People's Park and walked around Telegraph Avenue window shopping. Friends noticed that he seemed different. He started to push around a shopping cart filled with rocks, leaving piles of them here and there so that people would have something to throw when the revolution started. He enjoyed stopping traffic during rush hour and taunting the police. At the co-op in which he lived, he spent his days chipping at the cement driveway, with the intention of returning the man-made stone to nature.

Returning to his family home in Cupertino, Martinez gave up walking around naked. He continued studying judo, traveled to Europe, and tried to write a manuscript about his life, but he still acted erratically. Eventually, he was diagnosed with schizophrenia, and he spent the next decade in mental institutions and jails.

In January 2006, while living in a halfway house, Martinez got into a fight with a guard and was taken to the Santa Clara County jail. Further disruptions put him in solitary confinement in the maximum security section. The overcrowded jail offered minimal access to mental health professionals.

On May 17, 2006, Martinez was found by guards in his cell with a plastic bag over his head. He was rushed to the hospital, where he died the next day.

# Chapter 44

# From Russia, with Hate

## Nikolay Soltys—Sacramento

If there is any reason for stricter requirements for immigration to the United States, Nikolay Soltys is the poster boy. In 1998, the divorced Ukrainian émigré arrived penniless in the United States. He first lived in North Carolina before moving to Sacramento.

Sacramento County's Eastern European community numbers in the hundreds of thousands. It is a close-knit community of mostly fundamentalist Christians who have a deep distrust of police officers and banks—a carryover from the days of Communist Russia. Many of them stash their money at home, and this makes them vulnerable to home invasion robberies and extortions by their less scrupulous fellow immigrants.

Soltys received welfare and married another Ukrainian émigré, Lyubov. He showed his devotion to her by beating her frequently. What she saw in this psychopathically criminal and listless person will never be known. They soon had a son, Sergey, and, before long, another child was on the way.

Soltys never had a job, yet always had money. He was a thug who robbed family members of their welfare checks and their hard-earned money. He terrorized the Ukrainian community, committing extortion, racketeering, and auto theft.

On August 20, 2001, Soltys was supposed to start classes at American River Community College, but instead he stabbed Lyubov to death in their North Highlands home. Driving across town to his aunt and uncle's house in the Sacramento suburb of Rancho Cordova, Soltys stabbed and slashed seventy-five-year-old Petr Kukharskiy and seventy-four-year-old

Galina, along with their grandchildren, Tatyana and Dimitry, both nine years old.

Soltys then drove to his mother's house in another Sacramento suburb, Citrus Heights, and picked up his three-year-old son, Sergey. His mother later told the police that he appeared normal to her; however, considering the sordid life Soltys led in America, he probably did appear normal to her. Police suspected that Soltys changed clothes and washed off his relatives' blood at his mother's home.

The bodies of Soltys' relatives in Rancho Cordova were soon discovered, and the police began a frantic search for the killer and his child. Language barriers between family members and the police hampered the investigation. Slavic-speaking police officers from all over California quickly arrived in Sacramento to help translate and to build trust in the community.

Nobody will ever know what was going on in Soltys' sick and twisted mind when he drove off with his son. What is known is that Soltys drove to an isolated area in Placer County, lured his son into a cardboard box with new toys, and stabbed him to death.

Soltys' car was found in his old neighborhood, and police searched constantly for the crazed killer. After ten days, he was discovered hiding behind his mother's house and was arrested without incident. It was believed that he had been living in vacant houses in North Highland during the day and stealthily walking down railroad tracks to get food and supplies at night.

Soltys was charged with the murders of Lyubov, her unborn child, his son, aunt, uncle, and two cousins. While a guest at the Sacramento County main jail, Soltys gave himself a jailhouse tattoo and received minor injuries after jumping off of a second story tier.

Soltys' case was dismissed after he hung himself in his jail cell on February 14, 2002, Valentine's Day.

# Chapter 45

# The Gambler

## Frank Gambalie—Yosemite National Park

El Capitan is a three thousand-foot vertical drop rock in Yosemite National Park. The mountain is imposing in its massiveness and beauty. A favorite with mountain climbers, who come from all over the world to test their skills on the many challenging climbing routes, El Capitan shows no mercy for mistakes and stupidity. You are on your own when you are on the mountain.

Frank Gambalie was a resident of Zephyr Cove, Nevada, which is located three miles from the California state line at the east end of Lake Tahoe, but it is culturally part of California. Basically, if residents of Zephyr Cove need some-

### The Long and the Short of It

Yosemite National Park, a mecca for mountain climbers, has seen over one hundred climbers fall to their deaths while climbing the park's great stone walls. On October 15, 1968, James Madsen was on his way to help some climbers who were stalled on Dihedral Wall on El Capitan, when he rappelled off the end of his line and fell three-thousand feet. On July 25, 1972, climber Roger Parke was scaling Steck-Salathé on Sentinel Rock when he lost his holds and fell fourteen feet. Parke broke his neck and died. They were the longest and shortest fatal falls in Yosemite history.

## Youngest and Deadest

Seventeen-year old Irving Smith was attempting to be the youngest climber to summit Lost Arrow on March 19, 1960. He either rappelled off his rope, got tangled up in his gear, or became unroped, and fell six hundred feet, unwitnessed, wedging himself into Lost Arrow Chimney. His body was never recovered.

thing other than to lose their money at the casinos, they depend on California for their basic needs.

Gambalie got his kicks by BASE jumping. BASE is an acronym for Buildings, Antennas, Spans (bridges), and Earth (cliffs), from which participants leap, free-falling as long as possible before pulling their rip cords and sailing off in modified parachutes. Since this activity is illegal except with a special permit, there is an extra thrill of eluding the authorities upon landing.

BASE jumpers have to have a quick getaway plan or risk arrest, fines, and the forfeiture of their expensive custom parachuting rigs. The basic plan is to have several strategically placed waiting vehicles by which a jumper can escape. Another favorite is to have a decoy on the ground dressed as a jumper.

Gambalie, a well-known master BASE jumper and parachutist, was graceful in his jumps. Films of his parachuting skills show a fearless man gliding through the air as if it were his natural element. He would dance while in free fall, grabbing hands with fellow jumpers while they stood on each other's feet. Gambalie was a truly talented skydiver and BASE jumper. He had made more than five hundred jumps, at least nineteen of them off of buildings, including a successful early morning jump off of the Chrysler Building in New York City. After landing in that incident, he jumped into a cab and was in Brooklyn before the cops arrived. Gambalie was nicknamed "the Gambler" by his fellow jumpers. He vowed to never be arrested during a BASE jump.

BASE jumping is only allowed in national parks with a permit, which is never issued. The overworked park rangers have enough to do without having to tie up their precious resources retrieving dead or injured BASE jumpers from the talus. However, a trial run was granted from August 1 to October 31, 1980, and required jumpers to obtain permits, which were limited to a dozen a day, and only for El Capitan.

The experiment ended after sixty-eight days because of problems caused by the spectacle. Jumpers who could not get permits jumped anyway. Serious injuries, crowd problems, and ecological damage stressed the resources in the nation's third most visited national park. Rightly, the National Park Service saw that the wilderness value of Yosemite was losing out to a carnival atmosphere. The jumps attracted concentrated crowds that trampled delicate vegetation and caused traffic jams.

## Fatal Protest

Although Frank Gambalie did not die from BASE jumping directly, five BASE jumpers have died while jumping in Yosemite National Park. The last one was on October 22, 1999, just a few months after Gambalie drowned. Fifty-eight-year-old Jan Davis, in an act of civil disobedience protesting the Park's ban on BASE jumping, jumped off El Capitan and failed to release her chute. The sound of her impact set off car alarms.

Illegal protest jumps from El Capitan continued, much to the National Park Service's frustration. Four BASE jumpers died in accidents on Half Dome and El Capitan between 1982 and 1996.

On June 9, 1999, Gambalie made an illegal BASE jump off of El Capitan at 5:10 a.m. The jump was successful; however, the park service was tipped off by a camper on top of the mountain with a cell phone, and the rangers were waiting.

Landing in the west end of El Capitan Meadow, Gambalie was almost immediately cornered by two park rangers. Rather than admit defeat and allow himself to be arrested and fined for the misdemeanor and to lose his gear, the Gambler made a run for the roaring Merced River.

Dropping his gear, Gambalie dove into the Merced River, which was still running high with the spring thaw, and started swimming to the other bank. About halfway across the El Río de Nuestra Señora de la Merced, the current took Gambalie's strength away and sucked him under and down the river. The River of our Lady of Mercy showed the talented twenty-nine-year-old no mercy. He was found four weeks later, only three hundred yards downstream from where he was last seen.

# Chapter 46

## A Different Drummer

### Jim Gordon—Los Angeles

If people wanted to hear music before the invention of the phonograph in 1877, they had to either perform it themselves or find someplace where musicians gathered. In these modern times, listening to music is as easy as pressing a button. You can't avoid hearing it in shops, at work, or even as you walk down the street, and chances are that daily—if not hourly—you will hear a song featuring session drummer Jim Gordon.

Jim Gordon was born to play drums. In 1963, at the age of seventeen, the Los Angeles native was recording and performing with the Everly Brothers. His skills, all-American good looks, and solid work ethic made Gordon an in-demand session drummer. It was not unusual for him to take part in three different recording sessions in one day. He would often do multiple recording sessions in Los Angeles, then hop on a plane to Las Vegas to play drums for Andy Williams' or Mel Tormé's shows in Vegas' "big room."

Gordon played drums on such hit songs as the Beach Boys' "Good Vibrations," Glen Campbell's "Wichita Lineman," Carly Simon's "You're So Vain," and Seals & Crofts' "Summer Breeze." He played on most of the recordings by the Monkees and Bread, and he was the primary drummer on albums by mainstream artists like Cher, Jose Feliciano, Johnny Rivers, Manhattan Transfer, Nancy Sinatra, Harry Nilsson, Mama Cass Elliot, Randy Newman, Hoyt Axton, Neil Diamond, the Partridge Family, John Denver, Hall & Oates, Barbra Streisand, Barry Manilow, and the Captain and Tennille.

Gordon played drums with legends like John Lennon, Ringo Starr, George Harrison, the Byrds, Donovan, Gene Vincent, Linda Ronstadt, Eric Clapton, Alice Cooper, Jackson Browne, and Joan Baez. Country stars Merle Haggard, the Dillards, Van Dyke Parks, and Lowell George hired Gordon, as did bluesmen Lightnin' Hopkins, T-Bone Walker, John Lee Hooker, and B. B. King. Unconventional artists like Frank Zappa, Elliott Murphy, Hugo Montenegro, Nils Lofgren, Doug Kershaw, Jimmy Webb, and Leon Russell welcomed the straight-talking, buttoned-down, polite young drummer into their sessions.

As a twenty-one-year-old man making good money in Los Angeles' music industry in the late 1960s, Gordon had a nice car, a great apartment, and all the women he wanted.

But all was not right with the young man. Gordon would sometimes disappear for days at a time and come back in disarray. In those archaic days of psychology, most mental conditions that are now commonly diagnosed had not yet been defined, so nobody knows when Gordon started hearing voices in his head. It did not help that drug abuse among the era's musical stars was rampant. It was routine for the person booking a recording session to lay out huge lines of cocaine for his supporting

## The Curse of Derek and the Dominos

Jim Gordon is not the only member of Derek and the Dominos to have bad luck befall them. Eric Clayton's addiction to drugs and booze and the tragedy of the death of his son is well documented. A little more than a year after recording the album *Layla and Other Assorted Love Songs*, guitarist Duane Allman died in a motorcycle accident in Macon, Georgia, on October 1971. Besides being Eric Clapton's longtime bassist, Carl Radle recorded and played with George Harrison, Leon Russell, Dave Mason, J.J. Cale, Rita Coolidge, Art Garfunkle, Bobby Guy, Freddie King and on many 1960s pop songs as an uncredited session musician. Radle died at 37, on May 30, 1980, from a kidney infection brought on by years of alcohol and substance abuse. Keyboardist and songwriter Bobby Whitlock is the only member of Derek and the Dominos to have lived a life free from abnormal drama.

musicians to snort during the session. Gordon fell victim to the allure of the drug scene.

While touring with Delaney & Bonnie & Friends, Gordon met and befriended British guitar legend Eric Clapton. After the tour, Clapton grabbed Gordon, bassist Carl Radle, and keyboardist Bobby Whitlock from Delaney & Bonnie for his new project, Derek and the Dominos. After an English tour, the band retreated to Criterion Studios in Miami, Florida, to record the classic rock album *Layla and Other Assorted Love Songs*.

Early in the session, Clapton caught the Allman Brothers Band performing in Miami. Clapton, a huge fan of Duane Allman's guitar playing, was awestruck by his proficiency. He chatted with Allman after the show and drafted the renowned session guitarist into the band.

*Layla and Other Assorted Love Songs* turned into one of the first masterpiece double albums of the rock era. Anchoring the album is the rock classic "Layla," co-written by Gordon and Clapton. Legend has it that Clapton was unsure how to end the song, when he overheard Gordon playing the melancholic piano melody. It became the flowing coda of the song. Hefty doses of heroin, alcohol, speed, and cocaine during recording, along with Clapton's infatuation with George Harrison's wife, Patty, added to the heavy atmosphere of the album. The motorcycle death of Duane Allman and Clapton's escalating heroin habit put the band in limbo.

Gordon was continuously employed as a session drummer throughout the 1970s. He is listed as a performer on twenty-nine albums in 1973 alone. But toward the late 1970s, Gordon's mental illness became more significant. He started acting bizarrely at recording sessions, and the assignments trickled to a halt when, while playing drums for Paul Anka in Las Vegas, he stopped playing in the middle of a song and walked off the stage.

Institutionalized half a dozen times between 1977 and 1983, Gordon's mental health was often misdiagnosed as drug and alcohol difficulties. By 1980, Gordon was such a mess that he could no longer play his beloved drums. He was delusional, with his mother the focus of his disorientation.

On June 3, 1983, Gordon drove to his mother's home in Burbank and beat her to death with a hammer when she opened the door. Gordon was sentenced to sixteen years to life in prison. At this writing, Jim Gordon is incarcerated at the State Medical Correctional Facility in Vacaville and will probably never be paroled.

Gordon is one of the richest men in the California prison system, due to royalties from "Layla." He also receives a significant sum in royalties for his work with Traffic, George Harrison, John Lennon, and dozens of others whose golden oldies are played a thousand times a day.

In 1993, Eric Clapton's acoustic version of "Layla" received a Grammy Award. It is doubtful that the warden allowed Jim Gordon to display his award in his cell.

# Chapter 47

## The Panty King

### Roy Raymond—San Francisco

Roy Raymond was a smart man. You do not receive a Master of Business Administration degree from Stanford Graduate School of Business for not being one of the best and the brightest in the business world. In 1977, Raymond founded Victoria's Secret with loans from banks and friends, and he opened one store at the Stanford Shopping Center.

Raymond's idea was to sell lingerie in a setting that made men not feel like they are cross-dressers, by making them feel comfortable by employing sexy and friendly saleswomen who were there to help men pick out the right silk slips, lacy brassieres, and underwear. Business was so good that he opened three more stores and started a mail-order catalog with beautiful models tooling around in their underwear. The Victoria Secret catalog was a welcome parcel to receive in the mail, particularly for men who had their wonder years in the 1980s.

In 1982, Raymond sold Victoria's Secret, which included six stores and the catalog, to Les Wexner for between one and four million dollars. The sale was an amazingly bad deal, as the business was earning six million dollars a year. Yet Raymond was proclaimed as a business genius by the media for basically selling a catalog for millions of dollars.

Wexner, who founded The Limited clothing stores, took Victoria's Secret to new heights by expanding the stores into shopping malls throughout the world, creating name recognition that has cemented its place in pop culture. The company grew to over one thousand stores and the catalog ships 400 million copies annually. Victoria's Secret fashion shows are aired internationally and seen as an event in the world of fashion.

Raymond bought a big house in San Francisco and sent his children to expensive private schools. He enjoyed his newfound wealth and fame. Believing that he had the golden touch, Raymond started his next venture in 1984, a children's software retail store and catalog called My Child's Destiny.

By 1986, his new business was bankrupt. During the next few years, things got worse for Raymond when his wife divorced him and he had to face public shame when he could no longer afford his children's private academy tuition. For a guy with an MBA from Stanford, it was more than Raymond could handle.

On August 26, 1993, Ray Raymond walked halfway across San Francisco's Golden Gate Bridge and leaped over its side to his death. His body was pulled from the water a few hours later.

# Chapter 48

# The Tower of Wooden Pallets

## Daniel Van Meter—Sherman Oaks

Lifelong bachelor and eccentric Daniel Van Meter was born in San Francisco on March 3, 1913. His mother, Esther, was the great-granddaughter of President John Quincy Adams. His father was chemist James Van Meter, who invented the extremely toxic chemical compound cyanogen chloride, which was used effectively in the trenches of the Western Front during World War I. James was friends with the major scientists of the era: Thomas Edison, Nikola Tesla, Luther Burbank, and Guglielmo Marconi. Nobody knows if James brought cyanogen chloride home with him or if it had permeated his clothes and hair, but owing to his son's eccentricity, the odds are close to fifty-fifty.

During the 1930s, Daniel and his brothers, James and Baron, ran a chicken and goat farm at 2180 West Adams Boulevard in Los Angeles. The Van Meter brothers dabbled in offbeat, right-wing political associations and attended meetings of the pro-Nazi organization Friends of Progress. During World War II, Daniel, along with two of his four brothers, served time in San Quentin on charges of sedition under the Subversive Organizations Registration Act. They had not informed the government of their political affiliation. The conviction was reversed in a District Court of Appeals and the brothers were released without compensation.

The brothers eked out a living by working odd jobs and raising chickens, rabbits, and goats on a small ranch they bought at 15357 Magnolia Boulevard in Sherman Oaks in 1947. The area was fairly undeveloped at the time, and they combed alleys looking for recyclables and treasures. Eventually, their property was home to a junked city bus, ancient gasoline pumps, car parts, and a gun turret from a navy ship.

Brother Baron seemed to have a more stable life than Daniel. He became a square dancer and attended the National Square Dance Convention for fifty-one years in a row. Baron also collected beer cans and had one of the most important beer can collections in America.

An unabashed racist, Daniel had extreme right-wing political views. He believed that a war was being waged against Christianity, that the United Nations was a communist plot, and that California students were not being taught to think for themselves. Anyone who disagreed with him was a communist.

In 1951, Daniel heard that the Schlitz Brewing Company's Los Angeles plant had thousands of used 36″ x 36″ x 6″ pallets they wanted to get rid of. He called the plant and asked to have as many brought to his ranch as possible. Five truckloads showed up, carrying a total of two thousand pallets.

Daniel stacked the pallets in a concentric circle over the grave of a three-year-old boy who had been buried on the ranch in 1869, creating a beehive-like structure, with stairways along the edges. On top of the wooden wonder, twenty feet tall and twenty-two feet in diameter, was an opening thirteen feet wide, in which Daniel and Baron hung out, drank

## The Watts Towers

Between 1921 to 1954, Italian immigrant Simon Rodia built seventeen interconnected sculptures—including two that are almost a hundred feet tall—made of porcelain, glass bottles, rebar, scrap metal, and metal mesh covered in mortar. In 1955 Rodia got tired of the constant vandalism to his sculpture by local teenagers and gave away the property. Actor Nicholas King and film editor William Cartwright bought the property in 1959 for $3,000 in order to preserve it. In 1975, the city of Los Angeles received the property and in 1979 it was deeded to the State of California. It is now known as Watts Towers of Simon Rodia State Historical Park and is on the National Register of Historical Places and in 1990 was designated a National Historical Landmark.

beer, and watched the stars. Somehow the Tower of Wooden Pallets, as it became known, was classified as a fence by a building inspector.

The relatively country-like lifestyle the Van Meter brothers enjoyed was severely disrupted in the early 1960s when I-405 and US 101, also known as the San Diego and Ventura freeways, were connected with an interchange built near their property. Equipped with patio furniture and other comforts, the sculpture was still a place in which Daniel could find solace. The sounds of the vehicles on the freeways, two hundred feet away, turned into a soothing, surf-like sound.

In 1978, civilization started to close in upon the ranch. City fire inspectors declared that the tower was "an illegally stacked lumber pile." Van Meter was not a man to be fooled with. He approached the Los Angeles Cultural Heritage Commission and persuaded its council to designate the Tower of Wooden Pallets a Los Angeles Historic-Cultural Monument (HCM #184). The monument could stay until Van Meter moved or died.

Van Meter relished the publicity his folk art brought him. It gave him an audience

## The Hubcap Ranch

Italian immigrant Emanuel "Litto" Damonte retired from his job as cement contractor in 1942 and moved from San Francisco to rural Pope Valley, south of Middletown in Napa County. The primitive road that ran in front of his spread jolted hubcaps off passing vehicles, so the father of ten children started to hang the orphaned hubcaps on his fence, in case the owner came back to claim it. Before long Damonte had hundreds and then thousands of hubcaps, thanks to donations by his friends and neighbors. After two miles of fence was covered, he started covering his home, garage, trees, and outbuildings. Damonte, evidently bored with hubcaps, started mounting scrap metal, chains, tires, cans, and anything else that was bright and shiny. In 1987, two years after Damonte's death at age 85, the State of California deemed the Hubcap Ranch as a State Historical Landmark. The private residence is currently maintained by Litto's grandson Mike Damonte. The Hubcap Ranch is located at 6654 Pope Valley Road, Pope Valley, Napa County, California.

for his outlandishly racist views. Many news crews and journalists who had thought they were going to interview a grandfatherly eccentric were shocked by Van Meter's vile philosophy. Many editors killed articles on the Tower of Wooden Pallets because Van Meter's views were so repulsive. Television producers would save the day's work by creatively editing anything repugnant that Van Meter uttered.

Van Meter enjoyed being able to spew his whacked-out beliefs up until he died, in June 2000, at the age of eighty-seven. The Tower by then had collapsed and pancaked into a pile of rotting wood and rusty nails, and the land around it became condos and professional buildings. Until the historical designation was removed it was untouchable by land speculators.

Van Meter's heirs, who were often on bad terms with their uncle, were encumbered with not only the physical debris he left behind, but also a giant legal mess. The Tower of Wooden Pallets, rocked by earthquakes and ravaged by the hot southern California sun for fifty years, eventually stood only five feet tall. Yet because of the public art designation, permits had to be filed, and public meetings and detailed reports on the cultural value of the pile of broken pallets had to pass through the bureaucratic process before the Tower finally lost its landmark designation in 2006.

Van Meter's descendants received four-and-a-half million dollars for the property, and a ninety-eight unit condominium was built. There was no word whether the construction workers found the one hundred and thirty-seven-year-old skeleton of the three-year-old boy.

# Bibliography


Asbury, Herbert. *The Barbary Coast*. New York: Thunder's Mouth Press, 1933.

Atkinson, Janet Irene. *Colorful Men and Women of the Mother Load*. Sonora, CA: Jan Irene Publications, 2002.

Baldick, Robert. *The Duel: A History*. New York: Barnes and Noble, 1965.

Birmingham, Stephen. *California Rich*. New York: Simon and Schuster, 1980.

Buchanan, A. Russell. *David S. Terry of California: Dueling Judge*. San Marino, CA: The Huntington Library, 1956.

California Department of Parks and Recreation. *Five Views: An Ethnic Historic Site Survey for California*. Sacramento: California Department of Parks and Recreation, 1988.

Edelman, Rob, and Audrey Kupferberg. *Meet the Mertzes*. Los Angeles: Renaissance Books, 1999.

Gould, Milton S. *A Cast of Hawks*. La Jolla, CA: Copley Books, 1985.

Grey, Rudolph. *Nightmare of Ecstasy: The Life and Art of Edward D. Wood, Jr*. Portland, OR: Feral House, 1992.

Gutman, Bill. *Being Extreme*. New York: Citadel Press, 2003.

Haslam, Gerald W. *Workin' Man Blues: Country Music in California*. Berkeley: University of California Press, 1999.

Hayde, Michael J. *My Name's Friday: The Unauthorized but True Story of Dragnet and the Films of Jack Webb*. Nashville: Cumberland House Publishing, 2001.

Hornberger, Francine. *Mistresses of Mayhem*. Indianapolis: Alpha Books, 2002.

Howard, Moe. *Moe Howard and the Three Stooges*. New York: Citadel Press, 1977.

Imwold, Denise, and others. Cut!: *Hollywood Murders, Accidents, and Other Tragedies*. Hauppauge, NY: Barron's Education Series, 2006.

Lewis, Janice S., and Eleanor M. Ramsey. *A History of Black Americans in California*. Sacramento: California Department of Parks and Recreation, 1980.

Marinacci, Mike. *Mysterious California*. Los Angeles: Panpipes Press, 1988.

Maurer, Joan Howard. *Curly*. New York: Citadel Press, 1985.

McClung, Robert M. *The True Adventures of Grizzly Adams*. New York: Morrow Junior Books, 1985.

Munn, Michael. *Hollywood Rogues*. New York: St. Martin's Press, 1991.

Nash, Jay Robert. *Hustlers & Con Men*. New York: M. Evans and Company, Inc., 1976.

Nash, Jay Robert. *Zanies: The World's Greatest Eccentrics*. Piscataway, NJ: New Century Publishers, Inc., 1982.

Pendle, George. *Strange Angel: The Otherworldly Life of Rocket Scientist John Whiteside Parsons*. Orlando, FL: A Harvest/Harcourt, Inc., 2005.

Pitt, Leonard, and Dale Pitt. *Los Angeles A to Z: An Encyclopedia of the City and County*. Berkeley: University of California Press, 1997.

Pittman, Ruth. *Roadside History of California*. Missoula: Mountain Press, 1995.

Porter, Darwin, and Danforth Prince. *Hollywood Babylon: It's Back!* (Vol. 1). New York: Blood Moon Productions, 2008.

Reynolds, Ray. *California the Curious*. Arroyo Grande, CA: Bear Flag Books, 1989.

Richards, Rand. *Historic San Francisco: A Concise History and Guide*. San Francisco: Heritage House Publishers, 2003.

Roeper, Richard. *Hollywood Urban Legends*. Franklin Lakes, NJ: New Page Books, 2001.

Secrest, William B. *Dark and Tangled Threads of Crime*. Sanger, CA: Quill Driver Books/Word Dancer Press, 2004.

Secrest, William B. *California's Day of the Grizzly*. Sanger, CA: Quill Driver Books/Word Dancer Press, 2009.

Sifakis, Carl. *America's Most Vicious Criminals*. New York: Checkmark Books, 2001.

Sifakis, Carl. *Strange Crimes and Criminals*. New York: Checkmark Books, 2001.

Smith, James R. *San Francisco's Lost Landmarks*. Sanger, CA: Word Dancer Press, 2005.

Stanley, Leo. *Men at Their Worst*. New York: Appleton-Century Company, 1940.

Stern, Keith. *Queers in History*. Dallas: BenBella Books, Inc., 2009.

Wagstaff, A. E. *The Life of David S. Terry*. San Francisco: Continental Publishing, 1892.

Walker, Dale L. Eldorado: *The California Gold Rush*. New York: Forge, 2003.

Weaver, John D. *Los Angeles: The Enormous Village 1781–1981*. Santa Barbara, CA: Capra Press, 1980.

## Manuscripts and Journals

Ulrich Ruedel - Send in the Clones - Chaplin Imitators from Stage to Screen, from Circus to Cartoon

Joseph Pitti - California History Lecture Notes and Outlines - Volume's 1 - VI

Stephen Barber "Lyman Gilmore Jr. - Aeronautical Pioneer" Nevada County Historical Society, Volume 30, No. 2. April, 1976

## Newspapers and Periodicals

*Alturas Plain Dealer*

*Berkeley Daily Gazette*

*Corona Daily Independent*

*Los Angeles Examiner*

*Los Angeles Times*

*Fresno Bee*

*Sacramento Bee*

*Sacramento Union*

*Independent/Press-Telegram (Long Beach)*

*L.A. Weekly*

*Long Beach Independent*

*Long Beach Press-Telegram*

*Modesto Bee*

*Modoc Mail*

*Milwaukee Journal*

*Oakland Tribune*

*Pasadena Star-News*

*San Francisco Examiner*

*San Mateo Times*

*Time Magazine*

*True West Magazine*

# Index

# About the Author

*Amy Scott*

Born to first-generation Americans in Bay City, Michigan, **David Kulczyk** (pronounced Coal-check) is a Sacramento-based historian, freelance writer, and award-winning author of short fiction. He entered college at the age of 40 after working as a factory workers, sous chef, musician, warehouseman, fish butcher, process server, barista and bike messenger. Kulczyk's work has appeared in the *SF Guardian, The East Bay Express, The Chico News and Review, Maximum Ink Music Magazine, Madison Magazine*, the *Seattle Times, Pop Culture Press,* and the *Sacramento News and Review.* He is also the author of *Death In California: The Bizarre, Freakish, and Just Curious Ways People Die in the Golden State* and *California Justice: Shootouts, Lynching and Assassinations in the Golden State* (both available from Craven Street Books). Kulczyk lived in Seattle for most of his adult life, with stays in Austin, Texas; Columbus, Ohio; Madison, Wisconsin; and Amsterdam, Uitgeest and Limmen in the Netherlands. He has lived in Sacramento since 2002.

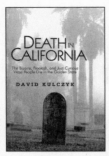

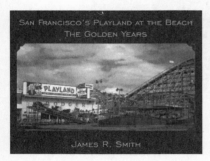